Technologies to Lead Schools

Technologies to Lead Schools

Key Concepts to Enhance Student Success

Edited by Gary Ivory and Dana Christman

ROWMAN & LITTLEFIELD
Lanham • Boulder • New York • London

Published by Rowman & Littlefield
An imprint of The Rowman & Littlefield Publishing Group, Inc.
4501 Forbes Boulevard, Suite 200, Lanham, Maryland 20706
www.rowman.com

6 Tinworth Street, London SE11 5AL, United Kingdom

Copyright © 2019 by Gary Ivory and Dana Christman

All rights reserved. No part of this book may be reproduced in any form or by any electronic or mechanical means, including information storage and retrieval systems, without written permission from the publisher, except by a reviewer who may quote passages in a review.

British Library Cataloguing in Publication Information Available

Library of Congress Cataloging-in-Publication Data Available

ISBN 978-1-4758-4492-4 (cloth)
ISBN 978-1-4758-4493-1 (pbk.)
ISBN 978-1-4758-4494-8 (electronic)

Contents

Foreword *Mónica Byrne-Jiménez*	ix
Preface *Gary Ivory and Dana Christman*	xiii
Acknowledgments	xvii
1 Principals and Teachers Empowering Teaching with Technology *Karin S. Forssell and S. David Brazer*	1
Key Points in This Chapter	1
Twenty-First-Century Instruction	2
Technology as Grease and Glue	3
Twenty-First-Century Assessment	4
Technology as Lens and Light	5
Supporting Teachers' Twenty-First-Century Competencies	5
Knowledge for Teaching with Technology	6
Technology Knowledge (TK)	8
Technological Pedagogical Knowledge (TPK)	8
Technological Content Knowledge (TCK)	9
Technological Pedagogical Content Knowledge (TPACK)	10
Building Teachers' Capacity to Use Technology	11
PCK: Focus on Teacher Expertise and Student Learning	11
Multiple Domains: Make Professional Development Suit Teacher's TPACK Needs	13
TK: Lower the Barriers to Teacher Learning	14
TCK: Make Tools Relevant	15
TPK: Make Learning Collaborative	16

	TPACK: Support Deep Understanding	17
	Context: Be a Bridge and a Buffer	17
	Make TPACK Your Own	18
	Conclusion	18
	References	19
2	Using Technologies to Instruct Students for Engagement and Thinking	23

Rosemarye T. Taylor, Janet B. Andreasen, Selma Powell, and Timothy Flynn

Key Points in This Chapter	23
What Is Scaffolded Instruction with Digital Resources?	24
Step 1: Introduction	26
Step 2: Guided Practice	26
Step 3: Independent Practice	27
Step 4: Assessment	28
What Does Digitally Scaffolded Instruction Look Like?	28
How Can Apps Facilitate Engagement in Learning and Thinking?	31
How Can Digital Tools Facilitate Student Collaboration?	31
How Can Digital Tools Increase Instructional Differentiation?	32
How Can a Leader Know Which Resources to Provide?	33
How Can the Leader with Limited Resources Provide One-to-One Devices?	34
How Can Principals Support Implementation of Digital Instruction?	34
Final Thoughts for Digital Instructional Leadership	35
References	35

3	Using Eduphoria *Aware* to Identify Student Academic Strengths and Weaknesses	37

Kevin Badgett

Key Points in This Chapter	37
Data-Driven Decision Making	37
District- and Campus-Wide Data	39
Grade-Level and Teacher-Level Interventions	39
Individual Students	42
Capacity Building	45
Conclusion	46
Reference	47

4	Understanding Legal Issues about Technology	49

Robert F. Hachiya

Key Points in This Chapter	49

Educational Law Issues: (1) Student Speech Rights	51
Landmark U.S. Supreme Court Decisions Related to Student Speech	51
Tinker v. Des Moines, 1969	51
Bethel v. Fraser, 1986	51
Hazelwood v. Kuhlmeier, 1988	52
Morse v. Frederick, 2007	52
Summary of Student Speech Rights	52
Educational Law Issues: (2) Student Search Guidelines	53
Landmark U.S. Supreme Court Decisions Related to Student Searches	53
New Jersey v. T.L.O., 1985	53
Probable cause vs. reasonable suspicion	53
Safford v. Redding, 2009	54
The Application of Student Rights and Student Misuse of Technology	54
The Important Distinction between On-Campus and Off-Campus Behaviors	55
The Application of Student Speech Rights and Social Media and Parody Threats	56
Educational Law Issues: (3) Student Bullying, Harassment, and Threats	61
Educational Law Issues: (4) Sexting	62
The Application of Student Rights Related to Searches of Electronic Devices and Monitoring of Student Social Media	63
Suggestions for Policy and Practice Related to Students and Technology	64
Considerations Related to Off-Campus-Generated Social Media Messages	65
Considerations Related to Matters of Threatening Speech	65
Considerations Related to Speech That Disparages Staff	65
Considerations Related to Speech That Disparages/Bullies/Harasses Students	65
Considerations Regarding Policy Issues and Student Handbooks	66
Conclusion	66
References	67
5 Using a Spreadsheet Pivot Table to Do an Equity Audit for Social Justice	69
Dana Christman and Gary Ivory	
Key Points in This Chapter	69
Social Justice, Equity, and Social Justice Leadership	70

Equity Audits	71
Using Percentages	72
The Excel Pivot Table	75
The Analysis	76
A Caution about Small Populations	83
Seven Steps toward Equity	84
Equity Traps	86
Equity Trap #1: Seeing Only Deficits	86
Skill Needed to Avoid Equity Trap #1	86
Equity Trap #2: Erasing Race and Culture	87
Skill Needed to Avoid Equity Trap #2	87
Equity Trap #3: Rationalizing Bad Behavior and Unfair Practices	87
Skill Needed to Avoid Equity Trap #3	87
Equity Trap #4: Norming the Negative	88
Skill Needed to Avoid Equity Trap #4	88
Aspire, Assess, and Move Forward	88
References	89
6 Technology, Ethics, and School Leadership	**91**
Scott McLeod	
Key Points in This Chapter	91
Four Ethical Paradigms	92
Scenario 1: Student Technology Access	94
Scenario 2: Student Technology Use	96
Scenario 3: Student Data Privacy and Commercialism	97
Scenario 4: Cyberbullying	99
Scenario 5: Sexting	100
Scenario 6: Curriculum, Technology Security, and Parent Opt-Out	101
Scenario 7: School Safety	103
Scenario 8: Student Learning and Credit Recovery	105
Scenario 9: Expectations for Educators' Professionalism	106
Conclusion	107
References	108
Glossary	**111**
Index	**117**
About the Contributors	**123**
About the Editors	**125**
About the Reviewers	**127**

Foreword

As a young teacher in New York City public schools, I remember attending a professional development meeting about "integrating technology" into our teaching. By that, what the administration actually meant was including the computer lab as one of the "specials" offered in the school. As part of the introduction, however, one thing was said that has stayed with me all these years: technology was defined as any "equipment" used in classrooms to foster learning.

The presenter, in an effort to allay our fears, stated that at one point the chalkboard and the pencil were new technologies that were introduced into classrooms and which, eventually, were so widely integrated as to be unnoticeable. In this sense the advent of computers represented the evolution of teaching technologies that could foster learning and become so ubiquitous in classrooms as to one day be unnoticeable. I found that inspiring and was eager to learn about how computers could strengthen my teaching.

Not surprisingly, in an overcrowded, low-performing urban school, the computers remained unplugged in their boxes and safe from little fingers for most of the school year. My students never got to use the computers and I never got to integrate technology into my practice.

It has been many years since I was a public school teacher. I have, though, been in enough classrooms, urban and rural, since then to know that all classrooms have computers—often in the back or sides of the room; most classrooms have access to the internet, and some classrooms have more interactive tools, like SMART boards—so the hardware is there.

In a 2010 NCES report on technology in public schools, survey results indicated that 100 percent of schools had "one or more instructional computers with Internet access" (Gray, Thomas, & Lewis, 2010, p. 2) and of those, "91 percent were used for instructional purposes" (p. 2). In addition, there was a 3 to 1 ratio of students to computers. While these results varied by community type and concentration of poverty in the school, they are, overall, encouraging. However, these statistics do little to shed light on how educators discuss, share, develop, and integrate technology into their practice or how these technologies foster learning.

In contrast to the positive statistics above, Du, Sansing, and Yu (2004) observed that what are often considered the "generic benefits" (p. 274) of technology in schools are actually distributed differentially by race/ethnicity and socioeconomic status. They found that whereas there was little difference between advantaged and disadvantaged student computer use in schools, there were significant differences in computer use at home, with disadvantaged students having less access.

Computer use *at home*, interestingly, was found to have a greater impact on achievement than use *in school*. Research on the stratification of technology use is clear in that "disadvantaged children, even with access to new technologies, are more likely to use them for rote learning activities rather than for intellectually demanding inquiries" (p. 275). Overall, students living in poverty and students of color benefited *less* from technology at school or at home.

There is, in my mind, a connection between my experiences as a novice educator, the continued definition of technology as access to hardware, and research findings of the differential benefits of technology in schools: the role of leadership. Early in the adoption of technology to improve instruction, the North Central Region Educational Laboratory (NCREL, 1997) identified several components of effective professional development for technology integration.

Among these were connection to student learning, curriculum-specific applications (not "apps"), collegial learning, and new roles for teachers. In addition to other structural issues, the support of the leader was seen as necessary. This component narrowly focused on the administrative vision for technology and student learning. NCREL largely ignored the leader's role in creating the schoolwide conditions—such as collegial learning and expanded teacher roles—that foster the successful integration of technology across the curricula, learning processes, and school structures.

We know now that the other components are unlikely to happen without school/district leaders promoting a systemic and systemwide discussion of technology as a powerful pedagogical tool to fundamentally change how knowledge is created and shared in order to enhance student learning. In other words, technology is, at its core, *disruptive* (for all we know, the chalkboard and pencil were equally disruptive in their time).

Technology is, at its core, about disrupting systems of learning in order to foster *equitable* classroom and outcomes. Without leaders embracing this fundamental aspect of technology we will continue to leave computers—and other technologies—in the back of classrooms, literally and metaphorically.

In the 2018 meeting of the World Economic Forum in Davos, Switzerland, Jack Ma, founder of the Alibaba Group (China's largest e-commerce company), urged attendees to rethink the way we teach. He stated that how and what we teach is based on a model that is two hundred years old. In other words, our educational "technologies" are outdated. It is worth mentioning that Mr. Ma, a former English teacher announced that he is stepping down as CEO of Alibaba to return to his educational roots later this year.

Technology, the "equipment" of education, has to enhance the very things that make us human: curiosity, creativity, and community. Technology is less about doing better and more about doing *different* so that all children can develop and strengthen the skills that will ensure their long-term success in an increasingly integrated world—where walls are irrelevant and our unique yet connected trajectories are enhanced. Educational leaders and researchers need to be at this crossroad asking questions, exploring new language and new possibilities, and connecting people and their hopes.

In 2000, Michael Fullan said that "the more powerful that technology becomes, the more indispensable good teachers are" (p. 4). The same can be said for educational leaders. And the same can be said for researchers and scholars in educational leadership. I applaud the editors of this book, Gary Ivory and Dana Christman, along with all the contributing authors, for standing at the crossroads and helping us ask, explore, and connect. ¡Adelante!

Mónica Byrne-Jiménez
Indiana University

REFERENCES

Du, J., Sansing, W., & Yu, C. (2004). The impact of technology use on low-income and minority students' academic achievements: Educational longitudinal study of 2002. *Association for Educational Communications and Technology.*

Fullan, M. (2000). The three stories of education reform. *Phi Delta Kappan, 81*(8), 581–584.

Gray, L., Thomas, N., & Lewis, L. (2010). *Educational technology in U.S. public schools: Fall 2008* (NCES 2010–034). U.S. Department of Education, National Center for Education Statistics. Washington, DC: U.S. Government Printing Office.

North Central Region Educational Laboratory (NCREL). (1997). *Critical Issue: Providing professional development for effective technology use.* Pathways to School Improvement, North Central Regional Educational Laboratory, 1997. Retrieved from http://www.ncrel.org/sdrs/areas/issues/methods/technlgy/te1000.htm.

U.S. Department of Education, National Center for Education Statistics. *Technology in schools: Suggestions, tools, and guidelines for assessing technology in elementary and secondary education* (NCES 2003–313). Technology in Schools Task Force, National Forum on Education Statistics. Washington, DC: 2002.

Preface

In 2017, the U.S. Department of Education's (USDE) Office of Educational Technology held out the hope that "technology can be a powerful tool for transforming learning. It can help affirm and advance relationships between educators and students, reinvent our approaches to learning and collaboration, shrink long-standing equity and accessibility gaps, and adapt learning experiences to meet the needs of all learners" (p. 3). We are inspired by that hope, and we assume that since you have picked up our book, you must be similarly hopeful. We see this book as a step toward fulfilling the dream. We have produced it mainly for campus leaders and graduate students aspiring to be campus leaders.

We have not found anyone who thinks attaining the goal of transforming learning will be effortless. Few worthwhile things are. Furthermore, education leaders probably cannot delegate the work to others, to "the techies" or "the IT geeks." The Office of Educational Technology (2017) notes,

> Leaders who believe they can delegate the articulation of a vision for how technology can support their learning goals to a chief information officer or chief technology officer fundamentally misunderstand how technology can impact learning. Technology alone does not transform learning; rather, technology helps enable transformative learning. (p. 42)

Nor can campus leaders assume that the crucial leadership to transform learning will be handled by state and district leaders. The on-the-ground decision making of campus leaders will profoundly affect how any initiative—local, state, or federal (including technology initiatives)—will play out. Researchers from the Netherlands described the situation of schools this way: "School organizations are faced with different, often conflicting demands, desires and expectations of stakeholders and mandates from the government" (Rikkerink et al., 2016, p. 223). We suspect that description will ring true with campus leaders in any country. An Israeli scholar (Shaked, 2018) wrote that schools answer to a variety of constituents and are pulled in different directions by those constituents. As we wrote in a companion book to this one,

> You, as an education leader, . . . may feel distracted by responsibilities to an assortment of people: students, teachers, parents, community members, other administrators and school district personnel, higher education institutions, and the public.
>
> In particular, you must respond to pressures from a number of federal, state, regional, and local agencies outside of your schools and districts. Thus, while aspiring to the highest ideals, you may feel incredible pressure, like a juggler, to keep all the balls in the air (different-sized balls, of different weights, moving at different speeds). (Ivory & Christman, 2019, p. xv).

Shaked (2018) argued that the effect of having to respond to a variety of demands simultaneously is that the principal becomes a "mediating agent who must walk the tightrope between inside desires and capacities and outside demands and expectations" (p. 519). Because of playing the role of mediating agent, principals (and any campus leaders), "unofficially play an active role in adjusting external policy to suit their own perceptions" (p. 519). In the words of Weatherly and Lipsky (1977), principals turn into "street-level bureaucrats." We agree, because it is simply impossible to keep all the balls in the air. We do not care how smart, energetic, or dedicated you are; you cannot do it all. None of us can. Therefore, you must prioritize.

And if you want to use technologies to transform learning, you must prioritize wisely and be well informed about technology issues and understand what is at stake in the decisions you make. The USDE's Office of Educational Technology (2017) put it this way: "To be transformative, educators need to have the knowledge and skills to take full advantage of technology-rich learning environments" (p. 5). Rikkerink and her colleagues (2016) noted, "Sustainability of educational reform depends highly on the willingness and capacity of teachers to change their understandings, behavior and action repertoire" (p. 224).

We would expand their claim to include not only teachers, but administrators, and even school board members, as the National School Board Association has recognized (National Center for Education Statistics, 2002). So if you want to lead with technologies to enhance student success, you must be ready to learn, to access the big ideas, the key concepts that will help you prioritize and make good decisions.

There are many places you might start or continue your learning. Professional conferences abound; Parra (2019) describes in our companion book how you might even use digital technologies to learn more about digital technologies. We hope this current book is another important source for learning how to lead with technologies. Most of the chapters address the big ideas, the topics to keep in mind as you prioritize and decide. All of the authors emphasize practical implications, by means of scenarios, examples, or real-world cases. We are impressed with and grateful for the learning that they show in their writings.

So, what do we offer you here?

In chapter 1, Karin Forssell and David Brazer review for us the *pedagogical content knowledge* (PCK) framework. Our understanding of PCK has been developing for nearly forty years and they remind us of what a useful lens it is through which to view challenges of teaching and learning. They introduce us to an updated version, technological pedagogical content knowledge (TPACK), describe TPACK in terms of some ambitious efforts to improve student learning and show how it can guide a leader's efforts to plan good professional development for teachers.

Then, in chapter 2, Rosemarye Taylor, Janet Andreasen, Selma Powell, and Timothy Flynn address a topic that should interest all of us: student engagement and thinking and offer us a four-step instructional model to foster engagement and thinking. As they describe the model, they list a number of technologies that can be brought into each step to enhance its effectiveness.

Kevin Badgett, in chapter 3 addresses a topic that will be familiar to many readers: data-based (or evidence-based) decision making. Decades of facing state-level accountability systems have focused our attention in this area. Kevin's contribution is to introduce us to an app, Eduphoria *Aware*, that can facilitate access to data and analysis of data and enable us to carry these data and analyses from place to place and situation to situation.

Any administrator or campus administrator must be alert to and sophisticated in legal issues, walking carefully the line between student safety and good order on the one hand, and student rights on the other. The best education leaders understand general principles of school law and how they are likely to play out in practice. Technology, for all its promise of transforming student learning, has blurred some lines and rendered questionable some of the general principles. Robert Hachiya offers us chapter 4 to refresh our memory of some of the principles, and he brings us up-to-date on legal developments. His explanations can make us more effective (and safer) decision makers.

We two editors have written chapter 5 to help readers think about equality of educational opportunity, particularly for groups that have often been marginalized. We take the practice of the equity audit, which will be familiar to some readers, and show how technology can help with such an audit.

In chapter 6, Scott McLeod offers a development of the key concept of ethics in the use of and leadership of technology. He presents four alternative versions of ethics and then discusses how they might be applied in nine different scenarios.

So welcome to our book. If you believe in education as we do and aspire to become a better education leader, you have our greatest respect. If you intend to work to transform education for children and teachers, we admire you. If you will bring the powers of digital technologies to your leadership role, we salute you. We hope this book provides you good ideas to illuminate your journey.

REFERENCES

Ivory, G., & Christman, D. (Eds.). (2019). *Leading with technologies: Improving performance for educators.* Lanham, MD: Rowman & Littlefield.

National Center for Education Statistics (2002, November). *Chapter 7: Technology integration, technology in schools: Suggestions, tools, and guidelines for assessing technology in elementary and secondary education.* Retrieved from https://nces.ed.gov/pubs2003/tech_schools/chapter7.asp#7b.

Office of Educational Technology. (2017). *Reimagining the role of technology in education: 2017 national education technology plan update.* U.S. Department of Education. Retrieved from https://tech.ed.gov/netp/.

Parra, J. L. (2019). Searching, curating, and networking: Set up the tools and develop the skills to make the modern web work for you. In G. Ivory & D. Christman, (Eds.), *Leading with technologies: Improving performance for educators* (pp. 55–75). Lanham, MD: Rowman & Littlefield.

Rikkerink, M., Verbeeten, H., Simons, R., & Ritzen, H. (2016). A new model of educational innovation: Exploring the nexus of organizational learning, distributed leadership, and digital technologies. *Journal of Educational Change, 17*, 223–249.

Shaked, H. (2018). Why principals sidestep instructional leadership: The disregarded question of schools' primary objective. *Journal of School Leadership, 28*, 517–538.

Weatherly, R., & Lipsky, M. (1977). Street-level bureaucrats and institutional innovation: Implementing special education reform. *Harvard Educational Review, 47*, 171–197.

Acknowledgments

When Rowman & Littlefield invited us to do this book, we asked contacts around the United States to suggest how technology could help school leaders do their jobs and get better at doing them. Our contacts introduced us to their contacts, and all of these people gave us great suggestions for our book design. We then invited educators around the United States to submit proposals for chapters, and we had other educators review these proposals and give us feedback and suggestions. Finally, we invited selected people to write chapters for the book.

We are very pleased with their work. We express our gratitude and appreciation to John Nash of the University of Kentucky for his ideas and support in the design of this book, and to three experts who reviewed an earlier version of this manuscript: Teresa Wasonga of Northern Illinois University, Will Place of Eastern Kentucky University, and Tom Koerner of Rowman & Littlefield Education.

We especially thank the authors for their enthusiasm in sharing their knowledge and inspiration, and their patience as we labored to synthesize their valuable contributions into a coherent work. We list authors and reviewers at the end of this book. Finally, we thank Maria Cristina Padilla for her editing and formatting work on the final manuscript and for her excellent contributions to the glossary.

Chapter One

Principals and Teachers Empowering Teaching with Technology

Karin S. Forssell and S. David Brazer

KEY POINTS IN THIS CHAPTER

- Technology can improve student learning if teachers use it well.
- Effective use depends on their professional development.
- Principals can use the *technological pedagogical content knowledge* framework (TPACK) to guide their leadership of professional development for effective use of technology.
- *Pedagogical content knowledge* (PCK) is the special knowledge that teachers develop, which reflects their understanding of how students of a given level and set of circumstances best learn a particular topic or concept.
- Into the PCK framework, TPACK integrates *technological knowledge*, knowledge of technological tools.
- The TPACK framework helps principals attend to different aspects of supporting teacher knowledge growth in ways that empower teaching with technology.

Technology causes great joy or severe heartburn for many school leaders. Whether bedazzled by a new device, annoyed at teacher resistance, pressured by members of the community to align with twenty-first-century skills, or dizzied by the range of choices for hardware and software, a key challenge is this: How do we ensure that use of technology enhances learning outcomes for students? In this chapter we focus on developing knowledge bases for effective technology use in teaching and on central factors influencing leadership decisions that help teachers access the power of technology.

We present the *technological pedagogical content knowledge* framework, commonly referred to as TPACK (Mishra & Koehler, 2006; Koehler &

Mishra, 2009). TPACK gives us a way to understand what teachers need to know in order to make effective choices about organizing learning with technology. By focusing on TPACK, we provide a lens for principals and other school leaders to consider how to approach technology opportunities and challenges, learning alongside their teachers how to choose and implement technology in the classroom.

To illustrate the multifaceted aspects of technology application in the classroom, we present vignettes, drawn from experience, that describe the types of knowledge that teachers and leaders must draw on as they strive to apply technology to teaching and learning challenges. Building from these examples, we provide practical insights into the critical knowledge domains that help principals in leading TPACK growth and development for more effective teaching and learning.

Integrating technology into teachers' work in meaningful ways involves many players and stakeholders. For ease of presentation, we focus on principals supporting teacher learning. The purpose of instructional leadership as it relates to use of technology is to improve the quality of classroom teaching. As instructional leaders, principals are an important source of motivation and support for teachers' learning, fostering collaboration among teachers so that technology can be applied to persistent teaching and learning challenges.

TWENTY-FIRST-CENTURY INSTRUCTION

Mr. Mozart[*] teaches a combined fourth- and fifth-grade class in a K–5 school that values cross-curricular projects and social-emotional learning. Aligned with the overall vision and mission of the school, Mr. Mozart puts the students to work on an opera unit at the beginning of each school year, engaging all in language arts skills (reading, writing, editing, public speaking), social studies (an ancient Greek myth), and performing arts (singing, music theory).

Mr. Mozart partners with the outreach program at a local opera guild. Two guild volunteers visit the classroom once a week for ten weeks. Together with Mr. Mozart, they help the students develop and produce an opera, which the students perform for their parents and for the rest of the school.

Students and parents agree it is one of the highlights of the school year. Photos and videos of the performances are shared with grandparents and scripts are pasted into scrapbooks. Mr. Mozart uses the activity to develop community in his classroom by requiring students to collaborate on a mean-

---

[*] The teachers described here are composite descriptions drawn from our work with many practicing classroom teachers. With his permission we thank Mr. Otak Jump, a true Mr. Mozart.

ingful joint effort (communication, conflict resolution, responsibility, empathy, problem solving). This is a big production with multiple learning goals and outcomes, with the overlay of wrangling nine- and ten-year-olds into a close-knit community.

TECHNOLOGY AS GREASE AND GLUE

Digital technologies are integral to many of the interactions in Mr. Mozart's opera unit. The specific tools used shift as new applications become available and affordable. For example, Mr. Mozart's communication with community partners is expedited by a web search for the guild's contact information, and subsequent emails with the volunteers, thus easing resource acquisition for the classroom. Basing the opera on a particular myth identified by Mr. Mozart, students write the opera's story after comparing multiple expert perspectives on the numerous details of the myth found online.

Their understanding is enhanced by exploration of various artists' visual representations of the myth, which they find through a safe-image search. The students share online documents in which they write lyrics collaboratively; they compose and record the music on an electronic keyboard; and the event program is designed and produced using word processing, a scanner, and a copy machine. The performance is captured on a digital camera, uploaded to an online server, and shared with parents over email through a private online community. These sharing processes bind together student learning and community engagement.

In cases such as Mr. Mozart's classroom, technology allows teachers to design and implement lessons that help students learn more quickly, more deeply, and more creatively than might be possible without technology. The networking power of technology helps to create coherence among the perspectives of the teacher, students, and families. Communication enhances everyone's understanding of what happened, how it was experienced, and what it means.

The challenge for the principal in this case is to support Mr. Mozart and his colleagues to develop rich new instructional units through facilitating technologies. In other cases, technology changes the role of teachers, focusing their attention on new problems and highlighting new opportunities to make a difference.

TWENTY-FIRST-CENTURY ASSESSMENT

Ms. Brontë teaches tenth-grade English in a large suburban school district. Students truly enjoy writing in her classroom, where she engages them in meaningful discussions and writing about topics that interest them. She does this using a wide range of activities, many of them asking students to reach new audiences or take different perspectives using digital tools.

For example, students collaborate to publish book reviews online in a class newsletter, hold debates with another class in an online forum, and compare written texts to movie adaptations. Students share their work from class with friends and family. Thus Ms. Brontë gives students writing assignments that stretch their thinking and are, in and of themselves, learning experiences. Assessing those assignments presents a challenge, however. Ms. Brontë searches for ways to discover what students already know and what they need to learn so that her choices of activities align with students' needs.

Over several years, Ms. Brontë has worked with colleagues to develop writing rubrics in which rows represent specific learning objectives and columns describe ratings for each objective, ranging from Mastered (4) to Absent (1). General descriptions fill each cell. Despite their efforts to create inter-rater reliability in their use of rubrics, Ms. Brontë and her colleagues have found it hard to apply the rubric rigorously. Ms. Brontë has noticed that she sometimes "fudges" where she places any given rating to get to the overall score she thinks a particular student deserves based on other information about the student that is not addressed in the rubric.

Recently, Ms. Brontë and the other English teachers have been working together using an online platform for grading and evaluating their students' expository writing. The teachers' insights into their students' work have been raised to a higher level with the adoption of a blind review process, coupled with predetermined comments that can be tracked across multiple classes and years. The samples that the teachers used for developing the rubrics are available at any time for them and other teachers to reference, providing opportunities for recalibration of expectations and scores.

After students have submitted their assignments online, Ms. Brontë and her colleagues review student work anonymously, double-grading 10 percent of the essays. Everyone is randomly assigned a few extra essays from another class doing the same assignment. They rate papers according to the rubric, adding prepared comments such as "nice use of supporting evidence" and "please pay attention to spelling." When all the papers have been graded, Ms. Brontë generates a report for the assignment.

These reports inform Ms. Brontë's next steps. For example, the report reveals that a few of her students need individual help learning to cite sources. She also examines the report with her colleagues, noticing that many students across all English classes are having trouble with thesis statements. The teachers decide to collaborate on a lesson to address this topic. Based on the first round of essays, they fine-tune the comments in the system, merging some and adding new ones. They also revisit the rubric to clarify areas where colleagues rated papers differently.

The process leads to a discussion of the various ways in which the teachers' own expository writing has been evaluated formally and informally in out-of-school contexts. Through the use of this tool Ms. Brontë has turned data into information, then into knowledge, and ultimately wisdom (Rowley, 2007) that she can use to improve her teaching and her students' learning.

TECHNOLOGY AS LENS AND LIGHT

A well-designed online rubric tool and database can provide examples on demand and provide ways for teachers to flag borderline cases for discussion. Once assignments are scored, a digital tool can facilitate new ways of "seeing" by providing graphic representations of the data, highlighting trends, and providing benchmark overlays based on past years or comparison groups. In cases such as that of Ms. Brontë and her colleagues, technology can extend teachers' and principals' understanding of the strengths and challenges of individuals and groups of students, providing new insights that inform classroom practices.

SUPPORTING TEACHERS' TWENTY-FIRST-CENTURY COMPETENCIES

Mr. Mozart's lesson is successful for several reasons. The supportive school community, the availability of robust digital tools, and his own professional expertise all contribute to a rich learning experience for his students. Similarly, what Ms. Brontë's team seeks to accomplish requires physical and organizational infrastructure, and a strong understanding of the ways in which the use of analytical tools impact their students' learning experiences.

In the next section, we take a closer look at the knowledge Mr. Mozart and Ms. Brontë draw on to navigate teaching with technology successfully. Our aim is to provide a framework for principals to use as they create the conditions for teachers to develop the expertise they need.

KNOWLEDGE FOR TEACHING WITH TECHNOLOGY

Teaching with technology has been referred to as a "wicked problem" (Koehler & Mishra, 2008, p. 3), full of interdependent and ever-changing variables. A wicked problem has no definitive "solution"; in fact, the only option is to "re-solve [it,] over and over again" (Rittel & Webber, 1973, p. 160). To employ new digital tools effectively in learning activities and student assessment, teachers need a flexible set of skills and knowledge. What they need to know depends on what learning outcomes they are addressing for students, at which developmental levels, in what context, and with what technological resources.

This "wicked problem" mirrors the complexity of teaching. In the late 1980s, Shulman began articulating differences between pedagogical knowledge (of students, their differences, and their development), content knowledge (of the subject being taught), and pedagogical content knowledge, or PCK (how to instruct and assess students in that specific subject). PCK is a professional expertise that includes an understanding of instructional strategies, assessment, curriculum articulation, students' development of knowledge, and a teaching philosophy in a content area (Grossman, 1990; Magnusson, Krajcik, & Borko, 1999; Shulman, 1986).

For example, a teacher with strong PCK in mathematics would recognize and address common student misconceptions in conical intersections, or would have a grasp of several strategies for teaching fractions, and that teacher would assess and instruct in a manner specific to the particular difficulties students in her school would encounter (Ball, Hill, & Bass, 2005). Thus PCK differs for each subject taught, and will also vary with student developmental level, special learner characteristics, and the teacher's pedagogical orientation.

Technological pedagogical content knowledge, known as TPCK or more often (and easier to pronounce) TPACK, builds on teachers' pedagogical content knowledge, PCK. In the early 2000s, many scholars were trying to make sense of the ways that new technologies were changing what teachers can do. They built on the existing PCK framework to help them talk about the expertise that teachers leverage when using digital tools to support learning across subject areas (Mishra & Koehler, 2006; Koehler & Mishra, 2009).

Sometimes PCK is visualized as the intersection between pedagogy and content. Overlapping technological knowledge (TK) with PCK, pedagogical knowledge (PK) and content knowledge (CK) yields three new intersectional knowledge domains (see figure 1.1):

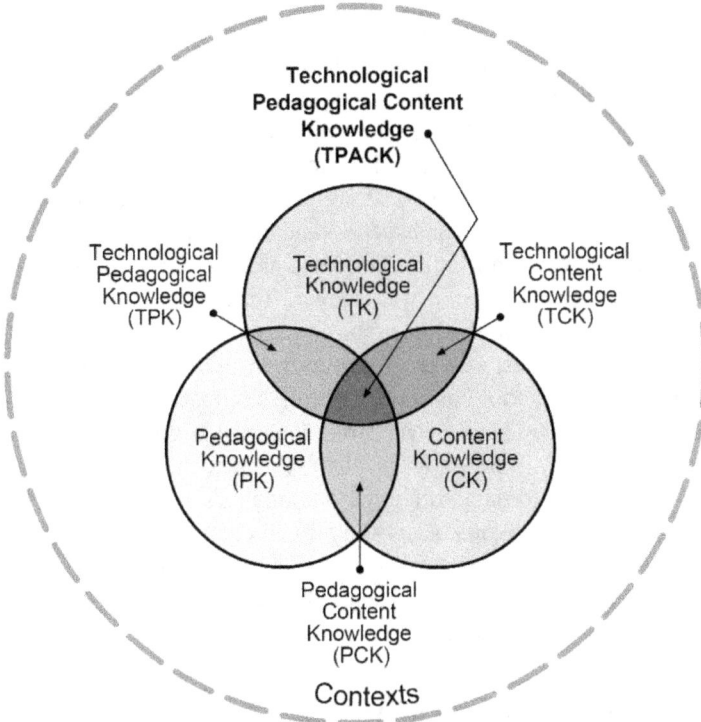

Figure 1.1. A Venn diagram representing the seven knowledge domains in the TPACK framework. (Reproduced by permission of the publisher, © 2012 by tpack.org.)

1. technological pedagogical knowledge (TPK)
2. technological content knowledge (TCK)
3. technological pedagogical content knowledge (TPACK)

In this chapter we address the domains included within the top "technology" circle and its intersection wth pedagogical knowledge and content knowledge.

We recognize that knowledge of tools, new and old, could be argued to be a part of PCK, rather than separate from it. However, treating technology knowledge as external to PCK is heuristically useful. The TPACK framework helps to ensure that a variety of possible needs are addressed and helps principals plan effective learning opportunities. Each of the technology-related terms is described in detail below.

Technology Knowledge (TK)

TK is the knowledge of the tool itself. Ideally, teachers would not need extra learning opportunities to learn to use the tool; it would be so "transparent"—the user would see right through the technology to the task at hand—that using the tool would come easily. The only decisions would revolve around when, where, and why to use which tool; the reasoning would be about which tool best meets the needs for instruction and assessment.

Unfortunately, new and unfamiliar tools are seldom so user-friendly that they require no learning curve whatsoever. Teachers who want to replicate Mr. Mozart's lesson will need some basic knowledge of how computers, the internet, digital cameras, and email programs work. Often they also need to know how to troubleshoot common software and hardware problems.

Meanwhile, teachers such as Ms. Brontë need to know what tools exist and where to click, drag, drop, copy, or paste. Further, those teachers who wish to apply technology to data collection and analysis will likely need to learn how to structure and use databases and how to create informative reports and charts. Teachers might also be asked to evaluate general usability of all of the tools at their disposal. The exact knowledge required will change constantly as new tools become available.

Technological Pedagogical Knowledge (TPK)

TPK is the knowledge of how students in a learning situation interact with technology. Mr. Mozart uses strategies for keeping his students on task in an online world full of distractions. He is aware of the range of prior knowledge extant among his students and uses that awareness to inform how he sets the requirements for the collaborative lyric-writing assignment edited by multiple students.

He knows that although the levels of technology use among this generation of students may seem high (Madden et al., 2013), so-called digital natives (Prensky, 2001) actually display significant differences in access patterns based on age, gender, family culture, and socioeconomic status. He keeps an eye out for students who have not yet learned the etiquette of social interactions online and gently includes those whose limited access to the internet at home makes searching for images unfamiliar.

He knows that the rich resources available to his students online come with a high price tag of distraction (Purcell et al., 2012). He works with his students to help them identify when they are off-task and recommends tools and strategies for engaging in focused work. Further, Mr. Mozart has developed knowledge of how to teach about ethics and acceptable use of technology and has established practices for managing digital equipment at the classroom scale.

Similarly, Ms. Brontë has learned how to guide her students through the use of the online submission platform. She knows that blind review is very different from the years-long refrain of "put your name at the top of your paper" and works to give her students an understanding of where to enter what information. She gives students time in class to review their comments on a larger screen, knowing that comments are harder to read on the mobile devices that many students rely on to access the internet.

Many of the strategies that fall into TPK are recognizable as a specialized subset of strong classroom management and course work organization. TPK addresses teaching methods, classroom management, assessment, and the connections among these vital components of classroom teaching and learning experiences.

Technological Content Knowledge (TCK)

TCK is a knowledge base closely tied to experts' use of tools in their content areas. Many fields have been impacted by the emergence of new technologies. Use of new tools leads to new interactions with content or visualizations of data, which in turn raises new questions in the field. For example, technology has altered the landscape for authors, as self-publication has become easy. In science, the development of new tools has made phenomena visible in ways never before possible. Central to TCK is recognizing how technologies are linked to developments in communication, in computation, or in sources of data in the natural or social sciences.

Mr. Mozart leverages his TCK in art when he discusses with his students how the advent of digital images has changed the experience of engaging with art across time and place. He taps more TCK in his ambitious opera project to teach students how the latest tools used by historians, writers, composers, and musicians combine to facilitate creation of a work of art.

This type of knowledge may impact classroom technology use more directly as students progress toward more expert practice. For example, advanced students may use the actual image creation tools used by experts, while younger art students may use applications that approximate those tools through simplified features and activities.

Ms. Brontë relies on her strong TCK in leveraging what she knows about the tools used by writers and how they have transformed the ways that professionals create, revise, and share their work. She understands how the online grading platform relates to the submission systems of real-world publications such as journals.

She is aware that the use of blind reviews has increased the number of women hired in symphony orchestras (Goldin & Rouse, 2000) and represented as first authors in journals (Budden et al., 2008), leading her to believe that this format may help students from a variety of underrepresented groups. She leverages her TCK when she uses online publication tools to motivate students to engage authentically in a community of writers beyond the classroom and when she teaches her students about how famous authors seek feedback when revising their work in progress.

Technological Pedagogical Content Knowledge (TPACK)

All of the above knowledge domains are relevant to using new digital tools for teaching. The final domain, TPACK, emphasizes the relationship of technology use to PCK. This is the special knowledge that teachers draw from in order to support students' learning of specific concepts or topics, leveraging the use of new technological tools.

Teachers with well-developed TPACK build on a foundation of PCK to find the ways in which new digital tools can add value to the learning experiences of students. Such teachers are focused on important learning outcomes, looking for tools that can help students achieve those outcomes more quickly, easily, or effectively. Without strong PCK upon which to build TPACK, a teacher may use technology to amplify poor teaching, for example, by making it easier for students to solidify misconceptions through uncorrected errors or losing the cohesiveness of a well-articulated curriculum by allowing students to jump from topic to topic without guidance.

Mr. Mozart's success in orchestrating a learning experience builds on his expertise as a teacher, expertise that spans history, literature, visual and performing arts, and motivation of preteen students. He leverages digital tools to extend and enhance the opportunities for his students to engage with the content and with each other.

Ms. Brontë already understands effective English/language arts pedagogy, including assessment. She enhances and expands her PCK through the use of digital tools. She recognizes that quick, objective feedback on writing is key to the learning process (Ervin-Kassab, 2017). Together with encouragement and support, timely constructive criticism changes the learning experience, especially for students who have lost trust in school (Yeager et al., 2014).

Ms. Brontë harnesses technology to make teachers' data use more prevalent and useful. She will use this foundation to challenge, interpret, and refine her use of the data as viewed through the digital system. With all these different types of knowledge relevant to effectively choosing and using new digital tools, what can principals and teachers do together to support teachers' development of the knowledge they need? The next section uses the TPACK framework to guide capacity building.

BUILDING TEACHERS' CAPACITY TO USE TECHNOLOGY

Schools face specific challenges influenced by the student populations they serve, the level of teacher expertise, expectations from their communities, and varying levels of resources. Consequently, rather than trying to recommend specific solutions to technological challenges, we offer and elaborate on basic principles that principals and their leadership teams might follow to lead instruction. We use the different knowledge domains of the TPACK framework as a launching pad to an overview of ways to support knowledge development, recognizing that strategies for one type of knowledge development may help with others as well.

Though we present them separately, these knowledge domains often inform each other (Koehler, Mishra, & Cain, 2013). And although we focus on principals, we endorse distributed leadership (Gronn, 2008), principals sharing responsibility and decision making to generate meaningful collaboration. Each of the principles listed below ought to be considered as part of the foundation for a comprehensive school plan.

PCK: Focus on Teacher Expertise and Student Learning

Considering technology use through the TPACK framework keeps the focus on the use of new tools to facilitate students' learning. All teacher professional development specific to technology integration should start with a clear understanding of the challenge or opportunity that motivates its use. Instructional leadership requires principals and other school leaders to recognize good instruction when they see it and to be able to design professional development experiences that enhance teaching and learning (Robinson, Lloyd, & Rowe, 2008).

The TPACK framework focuses on the responsibility of principals and teacher leaders to foster teacher learning in a manner that enhances the expertise of teachers, but with a twist: the leadership team must embody sufficient knowledge to understand the teaching and learning challenges that might be addressed by technology. Most important, they need to identify the type of professional development that will best serve individual teachers based on their expertise and goals.

Too often school personnel jump to solutions before clearly understanding the problem they are attempting to solve. This seems particularly noteworthy in the area of technology where there is often a "gee whiz" factor that drives technology adoption, that is, we can be so mesmerized by the power of the technology to do interesting things that we lose sight of the learning problem or opportunity we need to address. Identifying problems and figuring out which tools show promise for addressing their root causes requires organization and leadership.

Principals have a responsibility to focus teachers' attention on teaching and learning problems before they provide the means for teachers to learn how technology can help them. Additionally, teachers will be more likely to engage with tools that clearly meet a need. To be worth the investment of their time and effort, technologies must add value, whether by taking the place of less suitable or more expensive tools, amplifying positive existing practices to extend their reach, or transforming teaching and learning in ways that would otherwise be impossible.

The principals of the schools in which Mr. Mozart and Ms. Brontë work face divergent challenges with common threads. Instructional leaders need to focus first on teachers' PCK and the technologies that support learning. In the case of Mr. Mozart's opera, this is the kind of activity the principal would like to grow elsewhere in her school, but it would be impossible and undesirable to mandate that all grade levels put on an opera. The principal might choose to articulate the teaching and learning challenge as providing authentic, deeply engaging learning, thinking of the opera as but one example of how to get there.

Ms. Brontë's principal might consider how technology can support assessment that informs teachers' decisions about classroom practices across a variety of subject areas and levels. The commonality for all principals is that they want to help their teachers to use technology as a resource in their daily work in a manner that adds value. Rather than merely shifting tools, they need to exercise instructional leadership grounded in multiframe analysis of the structural and interpersonal elements required to design professional development that will lead to more effective teaching and learning (Bolman & Deal, 2013).

Multiple Domains: Make Professional Development Suit Teachers' TPACK Needs

Bringing teachers to the point where they can incorporate new technology into their practice requires building their knowledge in all these domains through professional development. How might school leaders create learning opportunities that meet the diverse needs of teachers in different subject areas, with different student populations, and with differing levels of comfort and experience using digital tools?

Understanding the competencies required for appropriate applications of technology in the classroom helps to target professional development that is effective for developing teachers' ability to use technology effectively. The leadership puzzle is figuring out how to help teachers cultivate the knowledge domains they need.

Technology use divorced from strong PCK will not support student learning effectively. Thus, for some teachers, the primary focus of professional development would be foundational PCK. Other teachers may be strong in their PCK, but lack an understanding of how to manage a classroom with technology (developing TPK). Still others may need to learn how to use technology to reach a particular set of students involved in learning a specific content (developing TPACK).

Professional development time and money is wasted when the approach is to put all of the teachers in a room for them to be "inserviced." Furthermore, the myths, stories, and symbols associated with one-size-fits-all professional development are so negative that an obviously different approach seems likely to convey more positive messages even before teachers experience the learning opportunity.

This is especially true with respect to technology because teachers' experiences, motivations, skills, and knowledge vary widely. The challenge of designing worthwhile professional development is compounded by the fact that both desired learning outcomes and available tools may change often. Rather than one-size-fits-all, a more nuanced approach to professional development is required. Consequently, principals and other instructional leaders will need to design professional development that is flexible and adaptable, both in the moment in which it is offered and as a program of capacity building over time.

For example, there are many levels to the learning that will need to be in place before other schools can emulate Ms. Brontë and her colleagues. First, there is the difficult task of establishing a shared understanding of what good student writing looks like, codified in a rubric (PCK). There may be a challenge determining what available digital tools best support rubric development, data collection, and analysis (TK/TPK).

Once they have made these decisions, the teachers must learn to assess and score student work, then how to turn data into knowledge about student progress (TPACK). This new information will lead teachers to consider implications for instruction, which may include insights about the limitations of one type of assessment and the need for multiple measures to understand students' full competencies (PCK). Thus, the use of technology may create needs for teachers to grow or refine their understanding of visualizations and data organization, or their assessment literacy, to comprehend their students' progress.

Choosing a tool and collecting data are relatively simple. Making sense of what has been collected, however, requires support from the principal in the form of professional development in data analysis and collaborative time for teachers to figure out meaning in the data they have collected. This is a slow and challenging process.

Ms. Brontë and her teacher team benefited from time to articulate clear learning objectives from the expository writing assignment, determining if the rubric they were using adequately addressed their objectives, then comparing data to figure out (a) if they were using the rubric reasonably consistently and (b) what they had learned about teaching and learning from their assessments. Any teacher team doing this type of collaborative analysis is likely to have differences that will need to be discussed in a climate of trust. It is the principal's responsibility to provide the time, the technology, and a variety of learning experiences.

TK: Lower the Barriers to Teacher Learning

Digital tools are constantly changing, so any learning about a new tool for teaching is learning with an expiration date. The goal is to standardize opportunity, not equipment. Different tools will provide solutions to different instructional challenges. Ideally, a teacher will be prepared to take up new tools as needed throughout the year and into the future. There is current agreement that job-embedded professional development is the most effective form of learning experience (Croft et al., 2010; Huffman et al., 2001).

This means providing learning to teachers as they need it. Principals should design structures for accessing and funding learning opportunities that teachers can use whenever they identify new needs related to teaching with technology, whether for evaluating or using a new tool (TK), generating novel pedagogical activities and structures (TPK), connecting with current technological advances in the subject area (TCK), or developing innovative practices for instruction and assessment (TPACK).

When meaningful learning problems have been identified and a technology-based solution emerges as promising, learning opportunities focused on the tool itself should be easily accessible. For tools with well-designed interfaces, the barrier will be very low. More complicated tools will require development of technological knowledge. Some teachers may need time set aside for following a tutorial or for exploration. For others, "playing" with technology can develop higher confidence in using it for teaching. Still others may need more guidance, working side by side with a more knowledgeable peer.

Note that making it easier for teachers to learn might mean investing in more expensive digital tools. Here our focus is on the cost in terms of teacher time for learning to use one tool as compared to another. Principals should be mindful of the hidden costs associated with tools that put a high burden on teachers. Teachers are not likely to develop advanced technical knowledge for all new tools, especially when the tools themselves are updated frequently. But they will engage with the tools that best address their teaching challenges and enhance student outcomes.

Principals can help teachers over inevitable hurdles they encounter as they work with new tools by providing a technical aide capable of making the machinery and software work when stalled by user error or other problems. If the technology is being used in a way that is truly valuable, then timely assistance is key to sustain teaching and learning benefits. Maintenance and troubleshooting support are vital to enhancing ease of use and thus keeping technology meaningfully adopted in classrooms.

TCK: Make Tools Relevant

Too often technology skills learned in professional development workshops are not applied to a meaningful and immediate problem relating to the work of teachers. Technology-focused professional development is more effective when targeted toward meeting teacher-identified needs. One approach to increasing teachers' capacity is to identify new tools relevant to the content they are teaching students.

To make technology use authentic, teachers will need to know how professionals in fields parallel to the content they are teaching would employ similar technology. We saw this in the Mozart and Brontë examples. Additional examples include research scientists using analytical or simulation software or professional sports teams using statistics stored in relational databases. This kind of thinking helps to make technology use more meaningful for teachers and students alike because they are engaged in "real" work rather than using academic apps that seem to have little or no connection to the world beyond school.

Teachers therefore require professional development that helps them to understand how professionals in a variety of fields use digital tools in their work. This knowledge is not likely to be available to most teachers because, for the duration of their professional lives, their field has been education. Principals can introduce teachers to relevant community members, provide salary advancement for summer work, and in other ways facilitate opportunities for teachers to connect with current tools and expert practices in the field.

TPK: Make Learning Collaborative

For regular (nontechnology) professional development, many schools structure themselves into teacher collaborative teams (CTs), often referred to as professional learning communities (PLCs) (Bauer et al., 2013). We suggest that this is a productive approach to learning about using new tools in the classroom as well.

Improving technological pedagogical knowledge (TPK) needs to focus on more effective organizing and managing of pedagogical activities. When teachers face challenges in their instruction, CTs provide a natural venue for discussing the effectiveness of specific technologies and the strategies for managing them. At the same time, teachers develop collective craft knowledge about technology applications. Embedded in the same school, colleagues understand community challenges, specific student needs, and local policies that constrain possible options. Within CTs teachers can share and build on each others' ideas and experiences.

The use of CTs to support TPK development comes with an important caveat. Job-embedded professional development can improve teaching and learning when teams engage in open inquiry and productive decision making and are fueled by expertise. But Cohen and Lotan (2014) remind us that "it is a mistake to assume that children, adolescents, or adults know how to work with each other in a constructive collegial fashion" (p. 41). There is nothing automatic about setting up teacher collaborative teams.

Interpersonal dynamics within CTs can lead to innovation in classroom strategies, or enforce the status quo, or even cause substantial discord. Thinking in human relations terms about small teams, principals will want to be sure that teachers know how to work well together (which, because of the isolated nature of teaching, cannot be assumed) and bring complementary skills and knowledge to their teams.

TPACK: Support Deep Understanding

Supporting growth in TPACK requires attention to the ways in which technology enhances or extends strong teaching and learning in a subject area. TPACK in math will differ from TPACK in art, or in science. TPACK for teaching at the first-grade level will differ in many respects from TPACK for teaching the same subject to ninth graders.

Teachers who report higher levels of TPACK also identify more people they can learn *from* and learn *with* (Forssell, 2011). Thus, it is not surprising that a great many strategies for developing TPACK involve collaborating with others (Harris, 2016). When teachers work in teams with similar interests, the teams become agile units for engaging in professional development focused on specific content or developmental needs. TPACK can be developed in teacher collaborative teams (CTs) organized by grade level, by subject area, or both, but they need substantial support to be be effective.

Furthermore, the principal ought to be clear with teachers in answering the question: collaboration for what purpose? If Mr. Mozart's principal is interested in encouraging teachers in her school to build from the PCK concepts embedded in the opera project, then she needs to provide guidance along with information and resources to CTs as they need it. Likewise, the principal in Ms. Brontë's school would need to find ways for other teachers to learn about rubrics, inter-rater reliability, and data analysis to make the best use of student performance data.

Brokering relationships is an important role for school leaders. The most effective CTs have important human resources upon which they can draw (Bauer et al., 2013). This suggests that the school leader identify the strongest teachers, those with the most PCK and TPACK, and enlist them to support those who seek to develop their TPACK. These teachers, with all or part of their assignments outside the classroom, are available to CTs first to understand a classroom challenge they are addressing, then to help them think through how technology might help and how they can transition to such technology.

Context: Be a Bridge and a Buffer

The TPACK of teachers is closely tied to the context in which they teach and learn. The open nature of schools as organizations is both an opportunity and a threat for principals and teachers. Despite principals' best efforts to control costs and allocate resources to make the best use of available technology, schools don't operate as closed systems; their walls are permeable (Scott,

2003). Principals who wish to sustain learning about and with technology play an important role, bridging to resources and buffering the school against threats (Scott; Pfeffer, 1981; Pfeffer & Salancik, 1978).

Opportunity comes in the form of access to resources, from the central office and from the broader community. Ms. Brontë and her team of tenth-grade English teachers benefited from a curriculum specialist's assessment expertise, a common central office resource. Her principal smoothed the way for teachers by identifying that opportunity and arranging for the specialist to attend meetings with the teachers. In other cases the principal has a role to play in sharing knowledge of community resources among teachers. Principals can learn a lot from Mr. Mozart's connections with various community resources, making them available to other teachers.

Threats can occur as outsiders strive to exercise control over processes or outcomes. For example, stakeholders in Ms. Brontë's school may be unhappy with reliance on subjective assessment of essays to determine students' overall grades. The principal should protect teachers from misunderstandings or threats that may emanate from parents, central office administrators, or the community at large while they work to develop their TPACK.

Make TPACK Your Own

With the rapid pace of technology change, principals also want to be mindful of their own development. Although principals cannot be expected to be experts in all content areas and related technologies, they should be conversant in teaching and learning over a broad range of topics (Brazer & Bauer, 2013; Stein & Nelson, 2003) and develop their TPACK so that they can provide technology expertise for their teachers (Chandra, 2016).

As they support teacher learning that enhances student learning, principals cannot merely be purveyors of professional development; they should also be participants in it. Instructional leadership is most powerful when principals engage in learning alongside teachers to gain a deep understanding of the changes they are striving to make (Robinson, Lloyds & Bowe, 2008). Principals are likely to see the best results when they develop their own TPACK.

CONCLUSION

The central challenge of technology integration is the development of teacher knowledge and organizational capacity to support development of teacher expertise. Because technology is always changing, this "wicked problem" is not going away. Ongoing, flexible, and well-supported learning opportunities must be put in place to meet this challenge. The TPACK framework helps principals attend to different aspects of supporting teacher knowledge in ways that empower teaching with technology.

We have brought together perspectives on teacher needs and capabilities with leadership imperatives to make a case for how to structure professional development that enhances instruction with technology. We suggest leadership teams work with teachers to choose tools that address specific teaching and learning needs, sometimes with individual teachers and often with small groups or teams. The goal is to help teachers identify a meaningful instructional challenge, and then to find, learn about, and use tools that address it. By managing and supporting teacher professional development such that it focuses on teaching and learning issues and technology applications, principals create an environment that supports adoption of helpful technologies, implementation of new ways of teaching, and appropriate and meaningful evaluation of student learning.

REFERENCES

Ball, D. L., Hill, H. C, & Bass, H. (2005, Fall). Knowing mathematics for teaching: Who knows mathematics well enough to teach third grade, and how can we decide? *American Educator, 29*, 14–22.

Bauer, S., Brazer, S. D., Van Lare, M., & Smith, R. G. (2013). Organizational design in support of professional learning communities in one district. In S. Conley & B. Cooper (Eds.), *Moving from teacher isolation to collaboration: Enhancing professionalism and school quality* (pp. 49–80). Lanham, MD: Rowman & Littlefield.

Bolman, L., & Deal, T. (2013). *Reframing organizations: Artistry, choice, and leadership* (5th ed.). San Francisco: Jossey-Bass.

Brazer, S. D., & Bauer, S. (2013). Preparing leaders: A model. *Educational Administration Quarterly, 49*, 645–684.

Budden, A. E., Tregenza, T., Aarssen, L. W., Koricheva, J., Leimu, R., & Lortie, C. J. (2008). Double-blind review favours increased representation of female authors. *Trends in Ecology & Evolution, 23*(1), 4–6.

Chandra, V. (2016). Understanding the role of a school principal in setting the context for technology integration: A TPACK perspective. In M. C. Herring, P. Mishra, & M. J. Koehler (Eds.), *Handbook of technological pedagogical content knowledge (TPACK) for educators*, second edition (pp. 235–245). New York: Routledge.

Cohen, E. G., & Lotan, R. A. (2014). *Designing groupwork: Strategies for the heterogeneous classroom* (3rd ed.). New York: Teachers College Press.

Croft, A., Coggshall, J., Dolan, M., Powers, E., & Killon, J. (2010). *Job-embedded professional development: What it is, who is responsible, and how to get it done well*. National Comprehensive Center for Teacher Quality. Retrieved from http://files.eric.ed.gov/fulltext/ED520830.pdf.

Davis, F. D., Bagozzi, R. P., & Warshaw, P. R. (1989). User acceptance of computer technology: A comparison of two theoretical models. *Management Science, 35*(8), 982–1003.

Ervin-Kassab, L. (2017). *The integrated A in TPACK: A model for investigating assessment through the technological pedagogical content knowledge framework.* Manuscript in preparation.

Forssell, K. S. (2011). *Technological pedagogical content knowledge: Relationships to learning ecologies and social learning networks* (Doctoral dissertation, Stanford University, Stanford, CA).

Goldin, C., & Rouse, C. (2000). Orchestrating impartiality: The impact of "blind" auditions on female musicians. *American Economic Review, 90*(4), 715–741.

Gronn, P. (2008). The future of distributed leadership. *Journal of Educational Administration, 46*(2), 141–158.

Grossman, P. (1990). *The making of a teacher: Teacher knowledge and teacher education.* New York: Teachers College Press.

Harris, J. B. (2016). In-service teachers' TPACK development: Trends, models, and trajectories. In M. C. Herring, P. Mishra, & M. J. Koehler (Eds.), *Handbook of technological pedagogical content knowledge (TPACK) for educators*, second edition (pp. 191–205). New York: Routledge.

Huffman, J., Hipp, K., Pankake, A., & Moller, G. (2001). Professional learning communities: Leadership, purposeful decision making, and job-embedded staff development. *Journal of School Leadership, 11*, 448–461.

Koehler, M. J., & Mishra, P. (2008). Introducing TPCK. *Handbook of technological pedagogical content knowledge (TPCK) for educators* (3–29).

Koehler, M. J., & Mishra, P. (2009). What is technological pedagogical content knowledge? *Contemporary Issues in Technology and Teacher Education, 9*(1), 60–70.

Koehler, M. J., Mishra, P., & Cain, W. (2013). What is technological pedagogical content knowledge (TPACK)? *Journal of Education, 193*(3), 13–19.

Madden, M., Lenhart, A., Duggan, M., Cortesi, S., & Gasser, U. (2013). *Teens and technology 2013*. Washington, DC: Pew Internet & American Life Project.

Magnusson, S., Krajcik, J., & Borko, H. (1999). Nature, sources, and development of pedagogical content knowledge for science teaching. In J. Gess-Newsome & N. G. Lederman (Eds.), *Examining pedagogical content knowledge: The construct and its implications for science education* (pp. 95–132). Netherlands: Kluwer Academic Publishers.

Mishra, P., & Koehler, M. (2006). Technological pedagogical content knowledge: A framework for teacher knowledge. *The Teachers College Record, 108*(6), 1017–1054.

Pfeffer, J. (1981). *Power in organizations.* Marshfield, MA: Pittman Publishing, Inc.

Pfeffer, J., & Salancik, G. (1978). *The external control of organizations: A resource dependence perspective.* New York: Harper & Row.

Prensky, M. (2001). Digital natives, digital immigrants. *On the Horizon, 9*(5), 1–6.

Purcell, K., Rainie, L., Heaps, A., Buchanan, J., Friedrich, L., Jacklin, A., Chen, C., & Zickuhr, K. (2012). *How teens do research in the digital world.* Pew Internet & American Life Project.

Rittel, H. W., & Webber, M. M. (1973). Dilemmas in a general theory of planning. *Policy Sciences, 4*(2), 155–169.

Robinson, V, Lloyd, C., & Rowe, K. (2008). The impact of leadership on student outcomes: An analysis of the differential effects of leadership types. *Educational Administration Quarterly, 44*, 635–674.

Rowley, J. (2007). The wisdom hierarchy: Representations of the DIKW hierarchy. *Journal of Information Science, 33*(2), 163–180.

Scott, W. R. (2003). *Organizations: Rational, natural, and open systems* (5th ed.). Upper Saddle River, NJ: Prentice Hall.

Shulman, L. S. (1986). Those who understand: Knowledge growth in teaching. *Educational Researcher, 15*(2), 4–14.

Stein, M. K., & Nelson, B. S. (2003). Leadership content knowledge. *Education Evaluation and Policy Analysis, 25*, 423–448.

Van Lare, M., Brazer, S. D., Bauer, S., & Smith, R. G. (2013). Professional learning communities using evidence: Examining teacher learning and organizational learning. In S. Conley & B. Cooper (Eds.), *Moving from teacher isolation to collaboration: Enhancing professionalism and school quality* (pp. 157–181). Lanham, MD: Rowman & Littlefield.

Yeager, D. S., Purdie-Vaughns, V., Garcia, J., Apfel, N., Brzustoski, P., Master, A., Hessert, W. T., Williams, M. E., and Cohen, G. L. (2014). Breaking the cycle of mistrust: Wise interventions to provide critical feedback across the racial divide. *Journal of Experimental Psychology: General, 143*(2), 804.

Chapter Two

Using Technologies to Instruct Students for Engagement and Thinking

Rosemarye T. Taylor, Janet B. Andreasen, Selma Powell, and Timothy Flynn

KEY POINTS IN THIS CHAPTER

- How can technologies enhance instruction to increase student engagement and thinking? We provide a scaffolded instructional model.
- Scaffolded instruction includes four steps: (1) introduction with direct instruction or guided inquiry, (2) guided practice, (3) independent practice, and (4) assessment. Digital technologies can be used at each step.
- We describe a sample lesson that uses the four steps.
- Finally, we offer advice on six challenges to using technologies effectively:
  - Making the most of apps to foster engagement and thinking
  - Using apps to promote student collaboration
  - Promoting differentiation of instruction with digital technologies
  - Deciding which digital resources to provide
  - Acquiring technologies in the face of limited resources
  - Supporting technology use as a principal

During two days in February 2014, we observed classrooms across grade levels and disciplines in a school in an affluent neighborhood. We noticed that neither teachers nor students were using digital tools in the learning process. As we debriefed with the teacher leadership team, they revealed their belief that if students were permitted to use devices, they would not pay attention.

At that point, a novice teacher meekly shared, "Although you all don't agree with me, I let students capture page images on their devices so they can participate, even if they forget to bring their books." To that admission, others responded that capturing images was cheating and indicated that they denied requests from students to use devices. These same teacher leaders maintained that the combination of rigorous standards, student lack of engagement, and time constraints made higher levels of student thinking impossible.

This scenario brings to light issues that teachers may raise (and that leaders should consider) related to implementation of digital resources. Our chapter addresses issues raised in the scenario: How do sound pedagogy and research-based instruction with digital tools, resources, and devices increase student engagement and thinking? First, we provide a scaffolded instructional model with digital resources, followed by an application in one of our classes (Timothy's). We then describe challenges of student collaboration and instructional differentiation, followed by digital examples and tools. Finally, we identify common challenges that principals may encounter and ways to address the challenges when implementing digital practices. Toward the end of this book is a glossary that defines some terms we use.

Accountability for student learning and expectations of increased rigor in the next generation of assessments are presenting challenges for leaders and teachers. To support efforts to meet these increased expectations, we provide practical examples of digital resources that we have observed to be effective in various learning environments. The digital landscape is rapidly changing, so our examples and advice are not the last word on the subject and may soon be replaced with better options. However, the resources and concepts for use of digital tools that we offer are grounded in research and have been observed to work with diverse teachers and students in varying school environments.

WHAT IS SCAFFOLDED INSTRUCTION WITH DIGITAL RESOURCES?

Leaders will find that teachers who implement research-based instruction and incorporate digital resources have better student engagement and higher levels of thinking as required for success on recently implemented standards, such as Common Core Standards. Teachers first need to identify the standard for students to learn. After identifying the target standard, they develop instructional plans that scaffold students from (1) introduction to (2) guided practice to (3) independent practice and then to (4) assessment that includes demonstration of mastery (Taylor, Watson, & Nutta, 2014). As the teacher proceeds through these steps, she reduces support as students move toward mastery of the standard. Throughout the sequence of instruction, the teacher is continually checking for understanding, clarifying misconceptions, and providing feedback to students.

The sequence of instruction in figure 2.1 begins with high teacher support during the introduction.

Figure 2.1 includes digital and nondigital examples for each segment of scaffolded instruction so that you can develop a mental model of instructional possibilities. Keep in mind that there are many other digital resources to consider and new ones that will emerge.

A misconception related to quality of digital resources is that with more action, information, and entertainment, more learning will take place. On the contrary, criteria for selection of digital resources should include that there are no distractors or extraneous information, or so much information that it may cognitively overload or confuse students (Mayer, 2001, 2008; Pass & Kester, 2006; Intentional Futures, 2015). Just as with print resources, digital resources should directly and clearly address the intended standards-based learning. We do not use them purely for the purpose of entertaining students.

Notice that figure 2.1 emphasizes feedback throughout. Digital tools can assist teachers in providing immediate, helpful, and generative feedback. We particularly highlight generative feedback, such as "What do you think would happen if . . . ?" (e.g., "we changed one variable?"; or, "the next president is an independent?"). Such feedback generates students' thinking for delving more deeply into the content being learned. Class digital spaces, such as those

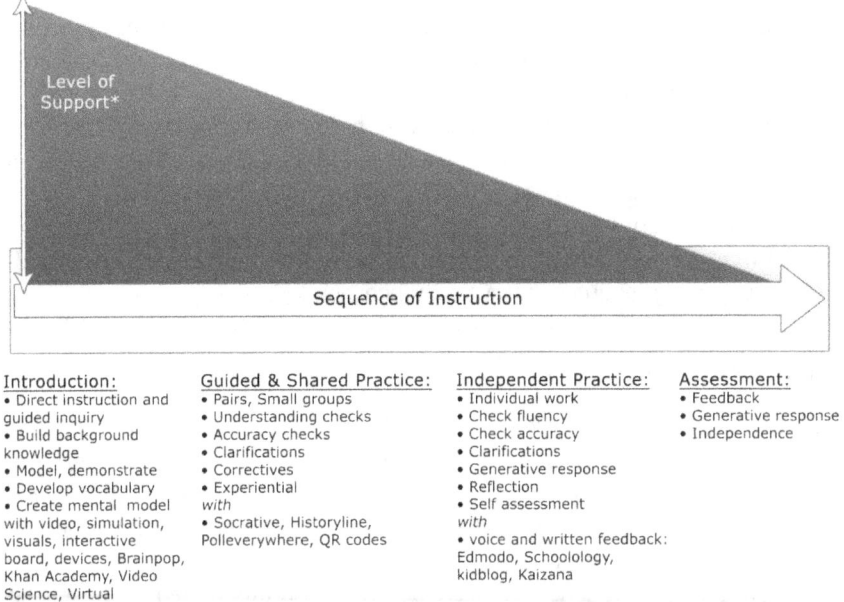

Figure 2.1. Examples for digitally scaffolding instruction for student success. (Based on figure 2.1, p. 12, in Taylor, R. T., Watson, R., & Nutta, J. (2014). *Leading, teaching, and learning the Common Core Standards: Rigorous expectations for all students.*)

that can be created in Edmodo and Google Education, are safe, private spaces that allow for teachers to provide detailed and helpful feedback.

In addition to providing more feedback, teachers can use digital tools to be more effective at checking for understanding during each of the four steps: (1) direct instruction or guided inquiry, (2) guided practice, (3) independent practice, and (4) assessment. For example, in this first step, without digital tools, it can be difficult to determine how many or which students understand the lesson introduction and are ready to move to guided practice. Student response systems, like Socrative and free or inexpensive applications (e.g., Poll Everywhere, Nearpod), use students' personal devices to check their understanding. With frequent and accurate information on student learning, teachers can quickly identify misconceptions, clarify points, and immediately reteach to identified needs, leading to more students being successful when they are assessed.

Step 1: Introduction

For students to develop quickly a mental model of their learning target, Mayer (2001; 2008) found that providing a verbal explanation and visual models simultaneously is effective. An introduction that aligns with Mayer's findings might include a YouTube video, Kahn Academy demonstration, Ted Talk (TED.com), or another virtual demonstration that introduces the target concepts and academic language.

Guided inquiry to increase students' thinking might follow, with students creating hypotheses or inferences based on evidences observed and heard. Alternately, a teacher might use inquiry by providing students an advance organizer with queries to engage their thinking before viewing and listening to either a virtual presentation or the teacher's presentation. Figure 2.1 provides other ideas and resources that may be incorporated.

Step 2: Guided Practice

As the lesson continues from (1) introduction (direct instruction or guided inquiry) to (2) guided practice, an instructor may incorporate digital resources to engage students' thinking to accomplish the learning tasks. Guided practice typically is collaborative so that students can learn from one another with the support of the teacher.

As an example, students may have been purposefully paired by the teacher. The teacher may ask pairs to complete an interactive Venn diagram to compare and contrast two concepts introduced during direct instruction or guided inquiry. These two websites (http://www.readwritethink.org/ and http://my.hrw.com/nsmedia/intgos/html/igo.htm) have many device-ready and interactive graphic organizers, like the Venn diagram, that are useful across grade levels and content areas. Student pairs either share with the rest of the class (think-pair-share strategy) or submit their completed graphic organizers to a safe digital class space (e.g., class Edmodo site).

Another example of incorporating digital tools in guided practice is to have small groups create digital flash cards of academic terms that include the word, a definition in the student's words, examples, and a nonlinguistic representation (Taylor, Watson, & Nutta, 2014). As in other examples, students can submit work, share work, and receive explicit and timely feedback from the teacher or peers in the class digital space.

We have found that text messaging during guided practice is another useful collaborative strategy. With text messaging, teachers are able to engage students and hold them accountable for their learning. Following is a reflection by one of us (Timothy) after using texting in U.S. History.

> This is a real observation that I've had. After I first introduced the activity (using text messaging as a learning resource), texting and off-task digital behaviors dropped dramatically. I didn't quite know how to introduce that concept. I pulled a few of my students aside and asked them about my observation. They confirmed what I'd observed, "We knew we'd be able to text during class so we just waited until the activity to do it."

In our experience, encouraging text messaging for collaborative learning projects has actually dramatically decreased off-task texting.

Step 3: Independent Practice

Recall that in our example of guided practice, students collaboratively compared and contrasted two concepts. During independent practice, students demonstrate mastery independently. But this is for formative evaluation rather than summative, that is, it is to identify ways to improve students' understanding and performance rather than to do a final check to demonstrate whether a standard has been met (Rossi, Lipsey, & Freeman, 2004). As with any assessment, students should receive feedback in a timely fashion that assists them in knowing these kinds of information: what they got correct and why, what they got incorrect, and how to make incorrect responses correct (Hattie, 2009). When students have demonstrated success independently, they are ready for assessment.

Step 4: Assessment

Assessment is always independent work by the student and aligned to the level of thinking of the standard. For example, if the standard is one in which students are to show knowledge of content, then the assessment would be at that same level (recall and comprehension). On the other hand, if the standard indicates that students are to analyze, then the assessment would require students to demonstrate analysis, for example, by comprehending and then taking apart the text according to the particular concepts being analyzed.

WHAT DOES DIGITALLY SCAFFOLDED INSTRUCTION LOOK LIKE?

Consider this social studies instructional plan implemented by Timothy in a high-needs diverse high school, but which could be adapted to any context (including to other grade levels and content areas). The plan includes the use of students' own devices.

The students are learning about the time period in U.S. history from the 1920s through World War II. The specific U.S. history standard to be addressed is: *Students will analyze the controversial New Deal policy*. They will demonstrate their mastery of this U.S. history standard through a writing standard: *Introduce precise claims distinguishing them from alternate claims. Create an organization that establishes clear relationships among the claims with reasons and evidence*.

In direct instruction, Timothy introduces President Franklin Roosevelt's New Deal policy with a brief two-minute video. Students view the video on their devices or on a classroom whiteboard. After the introduction to create the mental model of the New Deal policy, Timothy leads guided inquiry with the class to deepen understanding and check for misconceptions.

Next, in guided practice, students use their personal devices to scan five Quick Response (QR, see glossary) codes that Timothy has created in advance and posted around the classroom. These particular QR codes are linked to publicly available authentic documents from the Smithsonian Institution. The content of the documents presents arguments either for or against President Roosevelt's New Deal policy. Figure 2.2 shows an example of a QR code. QR codes can be created using a variety of free websites such as www.the-qrcode-generator.com or www.qrstuff.com.

Following the scanning of the QR codes, student pairs collaborate to complete the interactive Venn diagram by providing evidence-based arguments for and against the New Deal. The teacher reviews and provides feedback on the work of each pair, identifying faulty thinking or weak textual support

Using Technologies to Instruct Students for Engagement and Thinking 29

Figure 2.2. New Deal policy QR code

from the QR code sources. After collaboratively completing the Venn diagram, student pairs collaborate to write a five-sentence paragraph taking a position for or against the New Deal, supported with evidence from the QR code investigation and direct instruction. Students submit their work via a Google Drive document to receive immediate personal feedback from Timothy.

To differentiate instruction, those who are moving more quickly toward demonstration of mastery could then engage in a silent texting debate. A debate prompt is displayed on the white board to engage students' thinking beyond the standard. After the silent texted debate, students submit screenshots of their texted discussions via Google Drive for Timothy's review and feedback. Figure 2.3 shows a prompt and a one-screenshot example of two students' initial text at the beginning of the debate. Students' names and photos have been removed for anonymity.

In independent practice, each student uses his or her device to write three five-sentence paragraphs demonstrating analysis of the positive and negative perceptions of the New Deal policy. Each student draws his or her own conclusion, supported by evidence from the digital and print resources used.

After receiving feedback on their independent analyses and conclusions, students are ready for assessment. The online assessment is composed of multiple-choice items related to the New Deal. After responding to the multiple-choice items, each student composes a paragraph analyzing the positives and negatives of the policy and supports the claims with evidence.

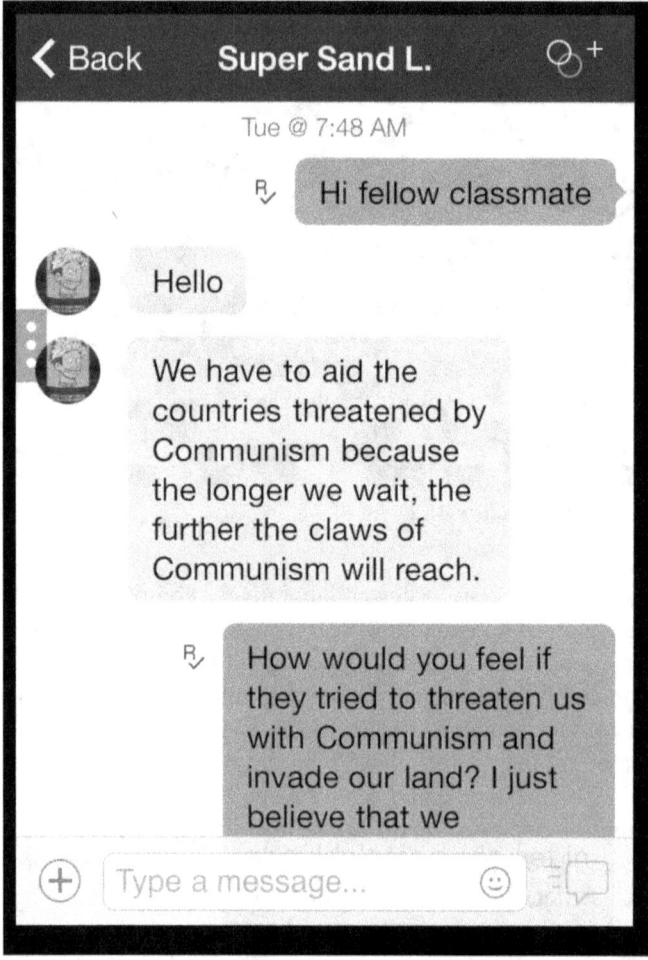

Figure 2.3. Authentic example of texted silent debate

HOW CAN APPS FACILITATE ENGAGEMENT IN LEARNING AND THINKING?

Implementation of digital resources can engage students, increase their thinking, and lead to increased classroom learning time. Applications (apps), some of which we have already noted, can provide systems for engaging students. Tools such as SplashTop or Doceri allow for remote control of a desktop computer by a tablet. Using SplashTop or Doceri, a teacher can control any program projected from a desktop computer when the teacher is in any location in the classroom. Not only does the teacher have proximity to students, but also the students can interact with the projected information or programs. For example, a mathematics teacher may have an algebra problem projected using PowerPoint. When discussing the solution, the teacher can allow specific students to solve the problem using annotations on the PowerPoint slide with a tablet connected with SplashTop or Doceri. Such practice increases student engagement and improves student management on the part of the teacher. No longer is the teacher tied to the desktop computer nor to the interactive board to control projected images.

Other apps, like Nearpod, allow the teacher to provide problems, presentations, or slides to students' own devices to increase engagement and thinking. Instead of projecting the learning task on a screen with a projector or interactive board, a teacher can use Nearpod to send the item to each student's device. Students respond or complete the work and submit it back to the teacher within an allotted time, again using Nearpod.

These kinds of apps can be used to check for understanding, to provide formative assessments, or to provide summative assessments. Digital resources provide a way to effectively manage students, increase instructional time, engage students, and increase students' thinking.

HOW CAN DIGITAL TOOLS FACILITATE STUDENT COLLABORATION?

Web-based apps can be used to facilitate student collaboration. Google Classroom can support student collaboration in problem-based learning, projects, and presentations. For example, think about students in social studies classrooms experiencing digital field trips without having to travel to specific locations (e.g., Google Earth). The same students may engage with students in other parts of the United States or the world to learn about culture, politics, government, or any other standard in the curriculum.

In a science classroom, students who are studying weather may use a Google Forms app to gather weather data from different parts of the country or world to analyze different weather patterns. Individual classrooms from across the country and around the globe can complete the Google Form each day with their weather data.

Through their global collaboration, students create a rich data set. All participating classes will have access to the data to analyze, draw conclusions, and make conjectures about weather patterns. They can create models about how the weather in one location impacts weather in another location. Students will have data to use as evidence to support or disprove the reasoned arguments they develop. In other words, they will think like scientists. Students may use apps like Pinterest to organize related information, including websites and ideas, prior to composing submissions that synthesize their findings and conclusions.

HOW CAN DIGITAL TOOLS INCREASE INSTRUCTIONAL DIFFERENTIATION?

Student engagement and levels of thinking can also be increased with digital tools through differentiated instruction. In collaborative teams, teachers can gather and examine student data in Google Forms. Through data examination, they identify needs for instructional differentiation within a class or across classes. They can then implement data-informed instructional differentiation with student groups to elicit higher levels of thinking from students who have already mastered the standard. As well, they can create groups of students who need more time, different instruction, or more support from the teacher.

Google Forms facilitates instructional differentiation. Information can be gathered quickly, related to how well students are progressing toward mastery of the standard or to identify concepts and content that are misunderstood. For example, a teacher can use Google Forms to create an exit slip or check-for-understanding that asks students to answer a specific question related to the day's learning target. Each student completes the form and submits his or her response. The responses are then accessible to the teacher through a spreadsheet, which includes timestamps and all information requested by the teacher. The teacher can then examine the spreadsheet data and identify patterns of progress and misconceptions. By using this kind of digital tool, teachers know which students need differentiated instruction and on which element of the standard. Teachers can respond quickly to needs they identify from student data.

One science example that may be applied to any grade or content includes the use of stations (Andreasen & Hunt, 2012). One group of students may be exploring the science concept of gravity by searching previously identified websites for information and applications. Another student group may explore the same concept using a digital simulation found on a professional organization's website. A third student group may complete an experiment that involves dropping objects while recording the time taken for the object to hit the ground (recording the investigation on their digital devices) and drawing conclusions based on the evidence gathered. A fourth student group may be with the teacher for greater support while viewing a virtual demonstration and gathering data on the same concept of gravity.

Stations can be implemented to differentiate instruction or to provide practice for all students. Students may be assigned to a particular station based upon student learning data (differentiation) or all may rotate through each station (guided practice, but not differentiation). Similar to the science example, the teacher can also be a station where (1) he fosters students' higher levels of thinking, (2) she clarifies difficult concepts or provides feedback, or (3) students who have mastered the standard may go beyond the standard. With the use of stations, digital resources enhance the possibilities for differentiation, engagement, and student thinking.

Instructors can use technology to adapt instruction in other ways to meet the needs of all learners, particularly those who are nonproficient or English Learners, or who have other unique needs. Examples, including text-to-speech options, are available on most tablets. Writers can use key-in or dictation software (e.g., Dragon Dictation) to compose paragraphs.

Additionally, software with fluent English reading of text is available to assist students who are visually impaired or who need a fluent model to develop oral language, fluency, and comprehension (e.g., nonproficient readers, English Language Learners). An example to engage even the youngest learners is digital storytelling. Shadow Puppet Edu (http://get-puppet.co) is a good example of a site with modeled storytelling. For older students YouTube's Spoken Verse has digital selections from classical and contemporary literature, all of which can serve to improve oral language, fluency, and reading comprehension (www.youtube.com/user/SpokenVerse).

HOW CAN A LEADER KNOW WHICH RESOURCES TO PROVIDE?

As a school leader you want to be certain that implementation of digital resources will increase student engagement and thinking, resulting in increased student learning. To help you identify the resources that most likely will bring this about, you may want to read *Learning Science & Literacy: Useful*

Background for Learning Designers, which was funded by the Bill & Melinda Gates Foundation (Intentional Futures, 2015). The report concludes that students learn more when identified elements, such as reducing extraneous information and using oral language narration along with visuals, are used in instruction with digital resources.

Also, you may want to consider professional organization websites that have specific content related resources and links upon which you can depend (e.g., International Literacy Association [ILA], National Council of Teachers of Mathematics [NCTM], National Science Teachers Association [NSTA], and National Council of Teachers of English [NCTE]). You are probably familiar with the Association for Supervision and Curriculum Development (ASCD), National Association of Elementary School Principals (NAESP), National Middle School Association (NMSA), and National Association of Secondary School Principals (NASSP). On these association websites you will find suggested readings about digital implementation and suggested digital tools for grade levels and across content areas. These sites also offer guidance for school leaders, with authentic examples from across the country.

HOW CAN THE LEADER WITH LIMITED RESOURCES PROVIDE ONE-TO-ONE DEVICES?

Keep in mind that students' use of personal digital devices is outpacing their use of school-provided devices. Digital-device policies that are flexible with respect to the digital device that may be used (student or school-provided) will accelerate implementation. Leaders who implement a "bring your own device" (BYOD) practice will want to make available school-provided devices for students who do not have personal ones. They will also want to provide support to those students who have not had digital devices and lack experience with them.

HOW CAN PRINCIPALS SUPPORT IMPLEMENTATION OF DIGITAL INSTRUCTION?

As a leader implementing digitally enhanced instruction, you will find that your school has to provide hardware, software, and related technical services. An on-site technical support person who can respond quickly to needs in any classroom is essential. In addition to the physical needs of digital tool implementation, there are also instructional needs. An identified digital instructional coach or coaches will be needed to support the effective instructional implementation of technology. Just as teachers learn their content and pedagogy, now they also have to learn which new tools and resources will be best for their context and how to use each to maximize student learning (see Karin S. Forssell and S. David Brazer's chapter in this volume).

Principals may find that it is beneficial to identify one or more model digital classrooms. Teachers can use planning periods to observe the model digital classroom teachers' use of digital resources, as well as ask questions of the observed teacher at a later date. Alternatively, teachers of the model classrooms may observe teachers' traditional lessons and immediately provide one or two specific examples of how to incorporate technology into the observed lesson.

FINAL THOUGHTS FOR DIGITAL INSTRUCTIONAL LEADERSHIP

Students and the younger generation of teachers think and process information differently from those in previous decades (Prensky, 2001). Engaging students as twenty-first-century learners in the classroom allows them to couple their interest in technology with learning, and therefore enhances engagement in learning. We hope this leads to increased classroom learning time.

To achieve these digital learning aspirations, leaders have to plan the introduction of digital resources, support the use of digital resources, and have patience as teachers find the ones that best suit their readiness, the student-learning standards for which they are accountable, and their students' individual learning needs. The well-informed leader will collaborate with and empower teachers to implement technology appropriately, monitor changes in student learning, and recognize effective digital teachers who can serve as resources to others. The digital instructional leader will see student engagement and higher level thinking when the school implements appropriate digital instruction.

REFERENCES

Andreasen, J. B., & Hunt, J. H. (2012). Using math stations for common sense inclusiveness. *Teaching Children Mathematics, 19*(4), 238–246.

Grissom, J. A., Loeb, S., & Master, B. (2013, October). Effective instructional time use for school leaders: Longitudinal evidence from observations of principals. *Educational Researcher, 42*(8), 433–444.

Hattie, J. (2009). *Visible learning: A synthesis of over 800 meta-analyses relating to achievement*. London: Routledge.

Intentional Futures. (2015). *Learning science & literacy: Useful background for learning designers.* Retrieved from http://www.meadowscenter.org/files/news/Learning_Science__Literacy_(iF_2015).pdf.

Khan Academy. (n.d.). Retrieved from: https://www.khanacademy.org/about.

Mayer, R. E. (2001). *Multimedia learning.* New York: Cambridge University Press.

Mayer, R. E. (2008, November). Applying the science of learning: Evidence-based principles for the design of multimedia instruction. *American Psychologist,* 760–769.

Pass, F., & Kester, L. (2006). Learner and information characteristics in the design of powerful environments. *Applied Cognitive Psychology, 20,* 281–285.

Prensky, M. (2001). Digital natives, digital immigrants. *On the Horizon, 9*(5), 1–6.

Rossi, P. H., Lipsey, M. W., & Freeman, H. E. (2004). *Evaluation: A systematic approach* (7th ed.). Thousand Oaks, CA: Sage.

Taylor, R. T., Watson, R, & Nutta, J. (2014, July). *Leading, teaching, and learning the Common Core Standards.* Lanham, MD: Rowman & Littlefield.

Chapter Three

Using Eduphoria *Aware* to Identify Student Academic Strengths and Weaknesses

Kevin Badgett

KEY POINTS IN THIS CHAPTER

- Eduphoria *Aware* is an application for analyzing and displaying data to support decision making.
- On a desktop or laptop, a leader can use *Aware* to analyze a variety of data and create data views. The leader can then use an iPad with *Aware* to share the analyses and data views with others.
- *Aware* is menu-driven and offers a variety of choices for selecting, disaggregating, analyzing, and displaying data.
- Optimal use of *Aware* depends on a commitment to evidence-based decision making and ongoing professional development.

DATA-DRIVEN DECISION MAKING

Instructional leaders need data to support their decisions about teaching and learning. Hollanders (2011) said that without data, you are just one more person with an opinion. The identification and use of relevant data can inform and substantiate decisions in all aspects of our job as school leaders.

In an age of emphasis on standardized testing, school leaders need tools that allow us to disaggregate data in order to isolate information relevant to decisions we face. While many school administrators have the ability to take large amounts of data and break it into digestible pieces, the task is time-consuming.

Furthermore, often we need to make a decision quickly and we cannot possibly carry our data binders around with us everywhere we go and quickly reference data pertinent to every moment and situation. Therefore, it is imperative that educational leaders identify and take advantage of tools to improve their efficiency, and ultimately, their effectiveness.

We need a tool that can provide analyses of data at a moment's notice. Eduphoria *Aware* is a subscription service that can help meet that need. With *Aware*, an administrator can gain quick access to a repository of preloaded data, including but not limited to, student performance on the state standardized exam, district benchmarks, grade-level exams, or teacher-created tests. In order to view desired information, the user sets parameters that, when applied, will produce data "views."

To take the greatest advantage of this resource, administrators will want to organize data in *Aware* to produce a "view" they anticipate will be most relevant to distinct conversations about student achievement and produce PDF copies of the corresponding reports on a desktop or laptop computer. Once the PDF file(s) is produced, the principal can upload that file to an iPad to support on-the-fly review in data meetings, IEP meetings, professional learning community (PLC) meetings or any other relevant setting. Because of the ability to produce these reports and save them for meetings, Eduphoria *Aware* supports a high degree of mobility.

With a district's paid subscription, accessing *Aware* is relatively simple. *Aware* is one of a suite of products offered by Eduphoria. After logging into Eduphoria (figure 3.1), one can select the option for *Aware* (figure 3.2).

After accessing *Aware*, you will have access to a range of information depending on your institutional role. As later screenshots will illustrate, there are district views, campus views, and teacher views. An individual's level of access is set by district leaders with the support of representatives from Eduphoria. Regardless of your role, the most natural place to begin a review of data is by looking at the Quick Views option in the *Aware* menu (figure 3.3).

After accessing the Quick Views link, you have a number of options for reviewing and analyzing the preloaded data. Preloaded data can be anything leaders decide will support formative and summative planning and decision making. As seen in the left side of figure 3.4, individuals can access District Assessments, such as curriculum benchmark assessments (CBAs). CBAs and other locally developed assessments are identified in *Aware* by a green pencil icon. Other assessments for which results can be stored include state standardized exams, teacher-created tests, and end-of-course exams. In this specific example, the CBAs are shown for each of four units at the fourth-grade level during the current school year.

Those with district or campus level roles can input new assessments and customize views by clicking the Edit button (figure 3.5). The title of the new assessment is below the Edit button (1) while figures 3.6 and 3.7 highlight options to access expandable menus in order to define data that will be aggregated from a new assessment.

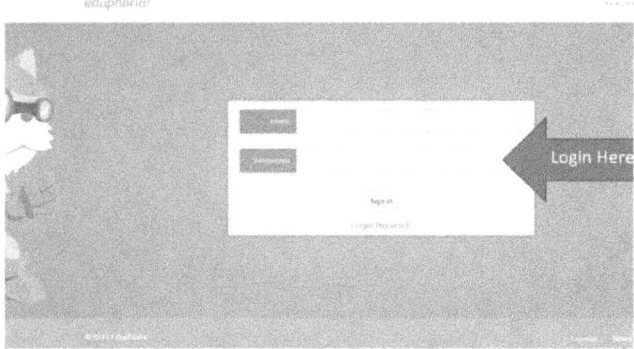

Figure 3.1.   Logging into Eduphoria (Kevin Badgett)

District- and Campus-Wide Data

For the remaining illustrations in this chapter, I will use dummy data from a standardized exam, the State of Texas Assessments of Academic Readiness (STAAR). Beginning at the district level, administrators can select campus-specific data. In addition to clickable links to whole-campus data, those with access can see breakdowns by demographic-group performance for any campus(es) within a district (figure 3.8).

Aware can show raw scores and derived scores. *Aware* also makes it possible for the school leader to review schoolwide performance on subtests and objective-level information assessed by an exam. In figure 3.9, these subtest scores are shown in columns titled R1, R2, and R3. Figure 3.10 shows student performance on individual learning standards.

Grade-Level and Teacher-Level Interventions

Campus leaders can further break data down to grade level and teacher levels. Doing so can support and inform whole grade, classroom, and small group interventions. Figure 3.11 demonstrates the use of *Aware* to review student performance within individual teachers' classes. As illustrated, one can also review student performance within various other categories. For example, across the top of the page, figure 3.11 shows performance on isolated learning standards. *Aware* allows educators to drill down into the data as deep as they want to go.

Figure 3.2. Eduphoria suite (Kevin Badgett)

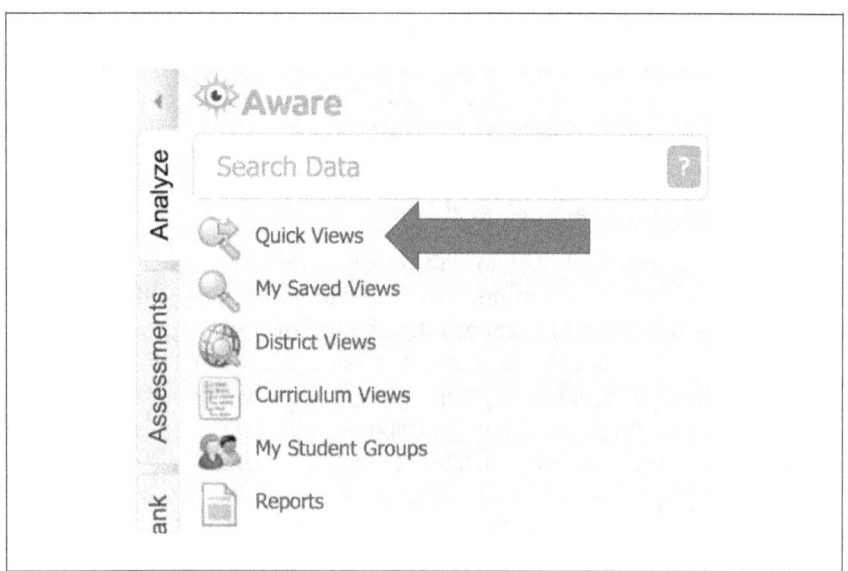

Figure 3.3. Quick Views option in the Aware menu (Kevin Badgett)

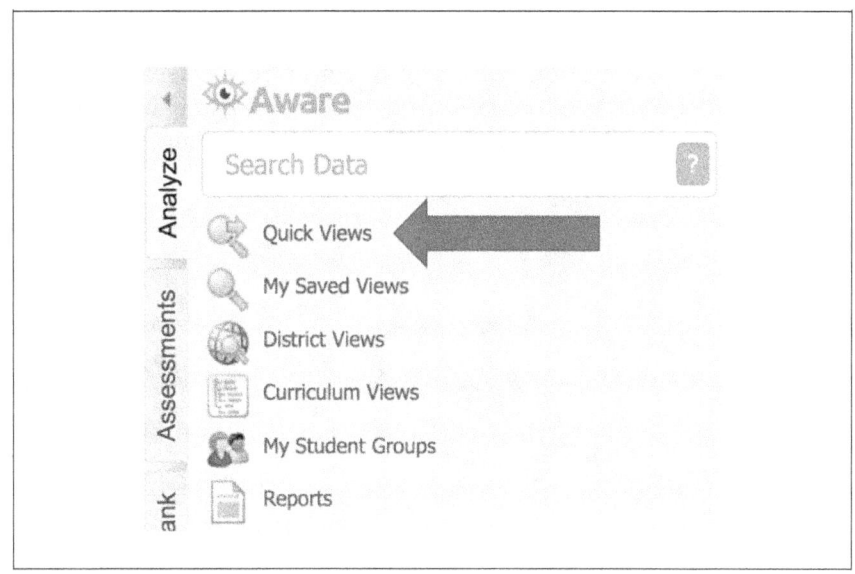

Figure 3.4. Access to District Assessments (Kevin Badgett)

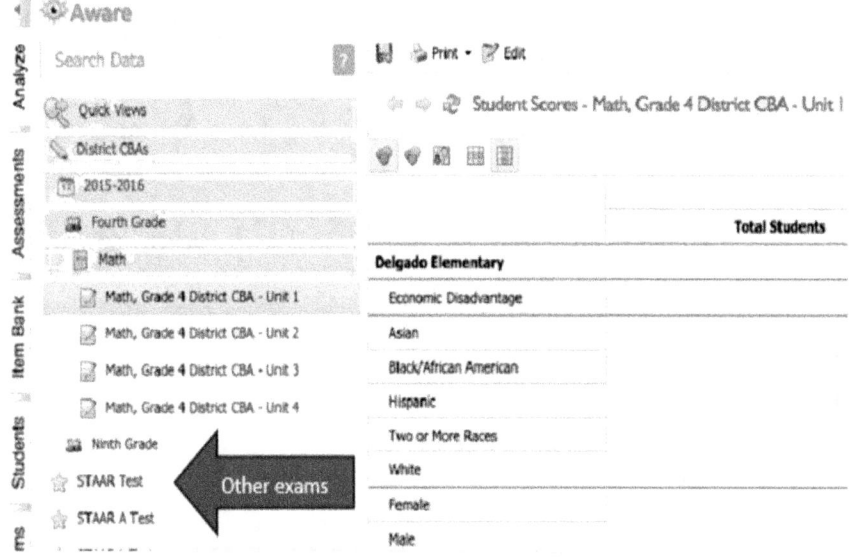

Figure 3.5. Title of the new exam (Kevin Badgett)

Individual Students

Though it is often most efficient to plan and instruct students in groups, there are times when we need to focus on students one at a time. Consider decision making in an Individualized Education Plan/Admission, Review,

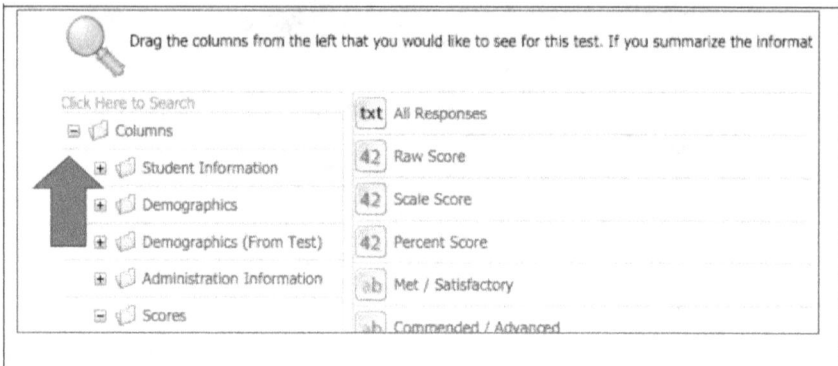

Figure 3.6. Expandable menu—Columns (Kevin Badgett)

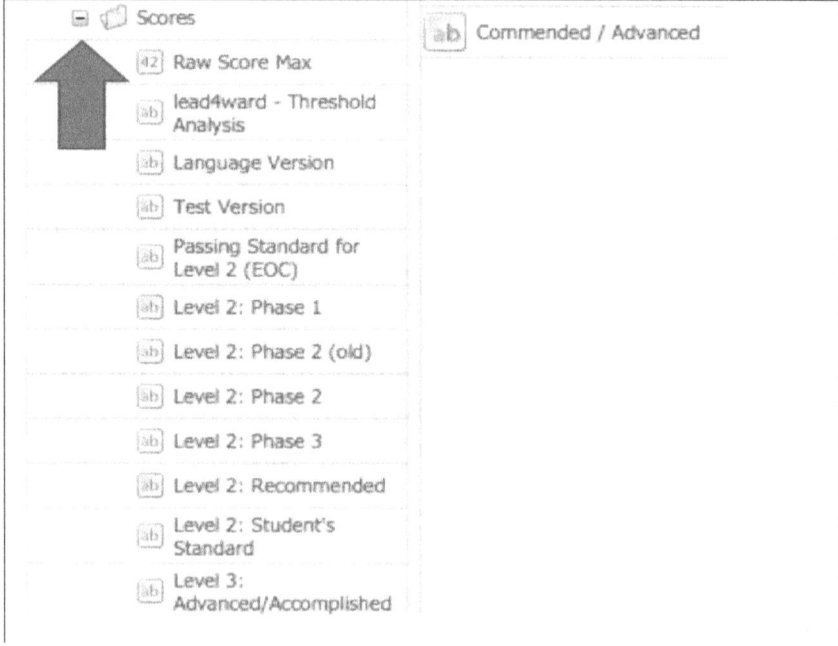

Figure 3.7. Expandable menu—Scores (Kevin Badgett)

Dismissal (IEP/ARD) meeting. Because we are making decisions about individual student needs, it is important that we have and use relevant and recent data tailored to answer questions about the specific student. *Aware* offers quick access to student-specific assessment performance information. This information can be based on data from a state standardized exam, a district benchmark assessment, a grade-level exam, or a teacher-created test. Access to these data can inform discussions about Present Levels of Academic Achievement and Functional Performance (PLAAFPs—descriptive statements about a student's current academic and functional performance),

	Total Students	Raw Score	Scale Score
Delgado Elementary	78	30.32	1521.35
Economic Disadvantage	18	29.50	1510.33
Asian	10	29.90	1516.50
Black/African American	3	33.67	1567
Hispanic	26	29.77	1511.38
White	39	30.54	1525.72
Female	33	31.82	1544.24
Male	45	29.22	1504.56
LEP	8	25.88	1454.25
Special Ed Indicator	4	22	1409

Figure 3.8. Access to demographic information (Kevin Badgett)

			All Categories	
	Total Students	R1	R2	R3
Delgado Elementary	78	72.56%	68.63%	66.04%
Economic Disadvantage	18	70.56%	56.22%	54.94%
Asian	10	74%	66.80%	64.60%
Black/African American	3	66.67%	79%	78.67%
Hispanic	26	69.62%	67.73%	65.46%
White	39	74.62%	68.90%	65.82%
Female	33	74.24%	72.94%	69.48%
Male	45	71.33%	65.47%	63.51%
LEP	8	63.75%	58.75%	55.13%
Special Ed Indicator	4	45%	63.50%	37%

Figure 3.9. Reporting categories (Kevin Badgett)

Figure 3.10. Learning standards (Kevin Badgett)

	Total Students	4.2(A) [R]	4.2(B) [R]	4.2(E) [R]	4.4(A) [S]	4.6(A) [R]	4.6(B) [R]
Delgado Elementary	78	79.49%	75.64%	89.74%	79.49%	69.87%	79.49%
Economic Disadvantage	18	88.89%	68.06%	88.89%	66.67%	66.67%	88.89%
Asian	10	90%	75%	100%	70%	60%	90%
Black/African American	3	100%	58.33%	100%	66.67%	83.33%	100%
Hispanic	26	65.38%	74.04%	88.46%	73.08%	67.31%	73.08%
White	39	84.62%	78.21%	87.18%	87.18%	73.08%	79.49%

Student Learning Standard Breakdown - April 2014 STAAR Reading, Grade 4

		4.2(B) [R]	4.2(E) [R]	4.4(A) [S]
Anderson, Julie		72.22%	72.22%	100%	83.33%
Economic Disadvantage	17	76.47%	72.06%	100%	82.35%
American Indian/Alaskan Native	1	100%	100%	100%	100%
Hispanic	14	78.57%	67.86%	100%	92.86%
White	3	33.33%	83.33%	100%	33.33%
Female	6	83.33%	54.17%	100%	100%
Male	12	66.67%	81.25%	100%	75%
LEP	12	75%	70.83%	100%	91.67%
Special Ed Indicator	1	100%	50%	100%	100%
Avary, KRISTYN	31	61.29%	68.55%	90.32%	83.87%
Economic Disadvantage	23	60.87%	66.30%	91.30%	78.26%

Figure 3.11. Breakdowns by individual teacher (Kevin Badgett)

development of goals and objectives, and recommendations for accommodations or modifications.

If there is a need to organize a new report in order to probe for possible patterns, data for individual students can also be imported into a report developed by the user. Figure 3.12 shows data for a small group of students. Included in the data for each student is information about individual demographics, a local ID, and performance relative to reporting categories, individual learning standards, and the student's performance on each individual test question.

CAPACITY BUILDING

Given that all teachers will have *Aware* access based on their roles, they can share in making data-based decisions for their students. However, to do this, they need to know how to access and use the data. To build teachers' capacity for instructional and remedial decision making using *Aware*, school leaders must provide training in how to use it. Such training should ideally be offered in an early and ongoing way.

Early training in the use of *Aware* should emphasize two areas of focus. (1) Make sure educators have training to select and analyze student achievement data. Otherwise, *Aware* is unlikely to be helpful. Teachers need to know what they are looking at and how the data they have can inform their teach-

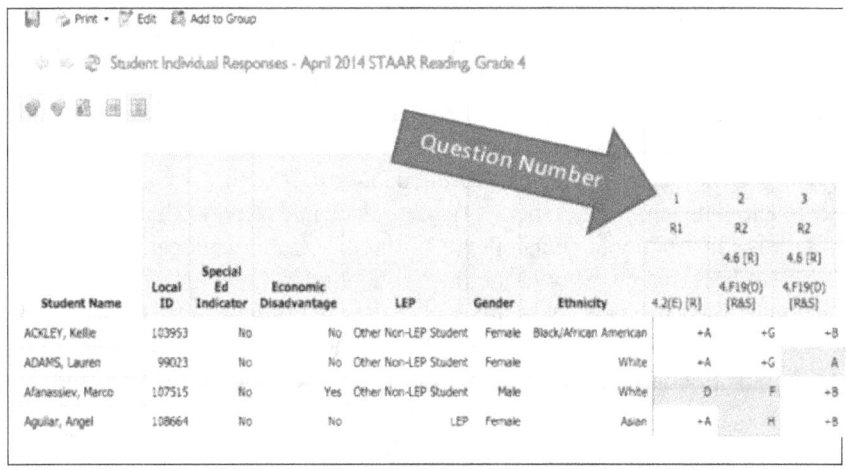

Figure 3.12. Student individual responses (Kevin Badgett)

ing. To diagnose student learning needs, they need training in whole group performance, subgroup performance, identifying patterns, and understanding how to move from examining data to diagnosing student learning needs.

(2) Anyone who will participate in evidence-based decision making should know how to produce and access reports in *Aware* and use findings to guide their decisions from the beginning of the school year. Not only teachers, but campus and district leaders can benefit from this understanding of *Aware*.

Ongoing training should focus on application. As new data sets become available through benchmarking, teacher tests, and ongoing state testing, these data sets should inform ongoing planning and action. While participating in various meetings that address student academic needs, school leaders can leverage available data and reinforce the importance of teacher use of *Aware* to inform their understanding of student academic needs.

When the principal becomes aware that a teacher is not using *Aware* effectively, this is an opportunity for one-on-one coaching and support or for faculty refreshers that can be offered during conference periods or in meetings before and after school. Regardless of how and when principals offer training to the teachers in the use of *Aware*, it is important. Without training and support, *Aware* will almost certainly become just "one more thing" we expect teachers to do.

CONCLUSION

Ultimately, everything done on a campus should be viewed through the lens of how it impacts teaching and learning. Therefore, it is vital that we identify and implement tools that support our ability to increase the leader's effectiveness as it relates to teaching and learning. While *Aware* is a remarkably helpful tool, it is only that: a tool. In determining whether and to what degree *Aware* is appropriate for their school, school leaders should consider specifically what use of *Aware* might add to their programs. A couple of the greatest benefits of *Aware* include the data-import repository and the ability to manipulate, organize, and reorganize data into reports that can support formative instructional decisions. Its portability from one location to another can also be valuable. Should the district determine there are other resources that meet their needs in these areas, *Aware* may not be helpful.

A second important consideration is whether or not priority can be given to an implementation process that prioritizes orientation in the use and support of *Aware*. Using any tool strategically is enhanced with a clear vision and knowledge that facilitates purposeful use. However, as valuable as this resource is, if a district has a greater priority in the moment, it may be good to delay the introduction of *Aware* as a resource that supports data-based decision making. Failure to shelter efforts and focus around prioritized initiatives can compromise procedural fidelity and, ultimately, hurt the overall effective execution of basic leadership responsibilities.

In closing, instructional leadership is central to the work of the school leader. However the school leader goes about the task of coaching and leading teachers in diagnosing and making decisions about student academic success, data should inform that process. For those without systemic tools and processes that support engagement in this task, *Aware* could be a helpful and valuable tool.

REFERENCE

Hollanders, D. A. (2011). Five methodological fallacies in applied econometrics. *Real-World Economics Review, 57*(6), 115–126. Retrieved from http://www.paecon.net/PAEReview/issue57/whole57.pdf#page=115.

Chapter Four

Understanding Legal Issues about Technology

Robert F. Hachiya

KEY POINTS IN THIS CHAPTER

- Education law related to technology issues in schools is an emerging and unsettled area of school law.
- When dealing with problems associated with misuse of technology, principals can rely on their basic foundational knowledge of student rights and their own obligations and responsibilities to maintain a safe and orderly environment.
- In this chapter, I review legal issues relevant to technology:
  ○ Student speech
  ○ Searches and seizures
  ○ On-campus versus off-campus behavior
  ○ Difficult issues such as student parody accounts and "sexting"
- Where the law is settled, I review the findings and implications. Where the law is unsettled, I provide guidelines based on relevant court cases and sound administrative practices.[*]

Principals face both good and bad news as they navigate the legal issues surrounding the use of technology in their schools. First, the *bad news*: cyber-related law with respect to schools is somewhat unsettled. Advancements in technology come faster than school policy can be instituted. For example, now principals must be concerned not only with policy surrounding the devices

---

[*] This chapter is intended as informational on the topic of legal issues and technology for principals and is not legal advice. If you are seeking legal advice you should comsult a licensed attorney in your state.

brought to campus that are owned by students, but also policy surrounding devices the school provides to students in one-to-one technology initiatives.

While the advancement of technology has positives for students and teachers that far outweigh the negative consequences, new technology generally brings new ways to misuse and abuse it. Practicing administrators understand that student misuse of technology is a frequent and time-consuming event.

The *good news* is that many of the problems that occur with student misuse of technology center around educational law issues principals should already be familiar with, including (1) student speech rights, (2) student search guidelines, (3) student bullying, harassment, and threats, and (4) student discipline related to violations of related policies. With the introduction of technology into a situation, principals may be unsure if such use alters the situation and how they respond. However, they should always refer back to their basic educational law knowledge, even when student use or misuse of technology has occurred.

For example, with regard to speech, new technologies allow for the more rapid and widespread delivery of various forms of student speech, but the basic speech rights of students—and the exceptions to students' speech rights—remain the same.

Also, new technologies allow for students to carry multiple types of devices, store multiple files, and have personal social media profiles. But the students' rights of privacy and protection from unreasonable searches, and the boundaries for school searches, remain essentially the same.

Additionally, new technology and social media have changed the nature and extent of bullying and harassment. But the requirements for schools to prevent and stop bullying and harassment have not changed.

The use of technology, particularly the use of social media by students, does introduce additional considerations that can create difficulties for principals. Although the issue of on-campus and off-campus behaviors has always been a concern for school officials, the fact that social media is virtually a 24-hour nonstop stream increases the chances of off-campus behavior becoming an issue at school. The very real problem of student sexting, even when done consensually, presents serious challenges for principals and other school officials.

A strong educational law background is useful for principals dealing with the student misuse of technology, but there are issues where courts have not always provided bright-line guidance, and sometimes it seems the courts are sending principals on an unguided walk through the woods. In this chapter I provide background knowledge on the rights of students in schools and guidance for how that knowledge can be applied to scenarios typically faced by principals. I also discuss policy issues with regard to teachers and technology. I offer guidelines for the development of responsible-use policies and practices to limit liability and keep students safer.

EDUCATIONAL LAW ISSUES: (1) STUDENT SPEECH RIGHTS

Landmark U.S. Supreme Court Decisions Related to Student Speech

Tinker v. Des Moines, 1969

Any discussion of education law that relates to technology and schools must begin with a brief review of the constitutional rights students have and the interpretation of those rights by the courts. The landmark decision in 1969 by the U.S. Supreme Court in *Tinker v. Des Moines Independent Community School District* famously noted that students do not shed their rights "[at] the schoolhouse gate" (*Tinker v. Des Moines*, p. 506, 1969). The Tinker case focused on symbolic, nondisruptive, and political speech.

The importance of the *Tinker* decision to the issue of balancing student speech and the responsibility of school officials to create a safe and orderly environment rests with what has become known as the "Tinker test." This two-pronged test says that school officials may only prohibit student speech that (1) causes, or reasonably could be expected to cause, material or substantial disruption of the operation of the school or (2) invades the rights of others.

The Tinker test is central to the problems associated with student misuse and abuse of technology. The questions we now face are these two: (1) Is particular student speech, which during an earlier era may not have been deemed to be disruptive to the operation of the school, now disruptive enough to warrant suppression? And (2) What is the impact of technology on the definition of schoolhouse gate?

Bethel v. Fraser, 1986

Another major U.S. Supreme Court case, this time one that carved an exception to student speech rights, was *Bethel v. Fraser* in 1986. In this case, a student presented a speech to the student body that essentially passed the two-pronged Tinker test because it did not cause nor could have been expected to cause a disruption, and it did not invade the rights of others; however, the speech was deemed inappropriate for the school environment.

The *Fraser* decision allows schools to limit student speech determined to be lewd, vulgar, or offensive. The court found that "vulgar and offensive terms" could be prohibited in schools because an essential part of the school's mission is to instruct children in proper values and society. One of the most frequently occurring discipline issues with student misuse of technology includes some form of speech that some consider to be lewd, vulgar, or offensive—even if the speech did not cause a disruption.

Principals must make judgments on a daily basis as to what words or actions may be deemed "vulgar or offensive," and must also determine if those words have caused or potentially may cause a disruption of the school or invade the rights of others, and thus, must weigh whether or not the words are permissible as constitutionally protected speech. When students misuse technology in various forms, especially through social media, principals must make decisions mindful of the speech rights students have and the exceptions courts have carved out from those rights.

Hazelwood v. Kuhlmeier, 1988

In 1988, in *Hazelwood v. Kuhlmeier*, the court ruled that school authorities could restrict speech where the school has a legitimate pedagogical interest. The court ruled in favor of a school principal who had prevented the publication of material in a school newspaper he felt would be objectionable to others.

Student speech on school grounds would generally be governed by *Tinker* or *Frasier*. But speech related to *school-sponsored publications or productions* would likely fall under the guidelines of *Hazelwood*, especially in cases where school officials are concerned the speech appears to be authorized by the school.

Morse v. Frederick, 2007

In 2007, a Supreme Court decision added *Morse v. Frederick* to what had been considered "the trilogy of student-speech decisions." The Supreme Court ruled in *Morse v. Frederick* that speech that could be considered promoting drug use could be restricted. In *Morse v. Frederick,* the court ruled narrowly against students who were disciplined for holding a sign that said "Bong Hits 4 Jesus" during an out-of-school activity. The court limited their decision to student speech that promoted illegal drug use, and for that reason, the holdings in the decision may not be relevant for principals dealing with technology use.

Summary of Student Speech Rights

It is helpful for principals to understand that the essential holdings of these student speech cases also apply to situations related to the use of technology. Understanding basic student rights and the circumstances that allow school authorities to limit those rights makes navigating potential problems associated with technology that much easier.

Principals should be mindful that their responses to student discipline issues affect the overall climate of the school—in terms of student expectations and behavior, the value placed on student freedoms, and the overall safety of all staff and students. Administrators should have justifiable reasons when considering interventions in student expression. The offensiveness of speech is not necessarily a justification for silencing or punishing the speaker. Caution should be exercised when disciplining speech that is not disruptive and speech that is political or has a particular viewpoint, even when such speech may not be popular.

EDUCATIONAL LAW ISSUES:
(2) STUDENT SEARCH GUIDELINES

An additional area of school law that principals must understand is that of governing student searches. Today school officials consider searches ranging from easy-to-conduct searches (e.g., students emptying the contents of their trouser pockets) to more complex ones (using metal detectors and trained dogs). Searches related to technology typically include searching for a device, but could also include searching the contents of a device or student-created content stored on a website or other storage platform.

Landmark U.S. Supreme Court Decisions Related to Student Searches

New Jersey v. T.L.O., 1985

In 1985, in *New Jersey v. T.L.O.*, the U.S. Supreme Court held that the prohibition against unreasonable searches and seizures applies to searches conducted in schools and during school activities. While the decision itself went against the student plaintiff, the court affirmed Fourth Amendment protections for students. In this case, the court overturned lower court rulings and concluded that the search of a student's purse was reasonable and held that the Fourth Amendment protections guarding against unreasonable search and seizure applied to searches conducted by school officials.

Probable cause vs. reasonable suspicion

Police searches are governed by a *probable cause* standard that must be met in order to conduct a lawful search. T.L.O. sued the school district arguing that the school authorities had neither probable cause nor a warrant to search her purse. The question became whether school authorities must meet the same standard as law enforcement when conducting a student search.

The Supreme Court ruled that school authorities can search students without meeting the high standard of probable cause that law enforcement personnel must meet. As long as they can meet the lower standard of *reasonable suspicion* they can conduct a search.

A student search must be justified at its inception, however, "when there are reasonable grounds for suspecting that the search will turn up evidence that the student has violated or is violating either the law or rules of the school" (*New Jersey v. T.L.O.*, p. 342, 1985). Once the initiation of the search is justified, it must be reasonable in scope, "when the measures adopted are reasonably related to the objectives of the search and not excessively intrusive in light of the age and sex of the student and the nature of the infraction" (p. 346).

The *T.L.O.* decision requires that school officials must have reasonable grounds to believe that the search of a specific individual will produce relevant evidence that a specific rule or law has been violated by the individual. Searches under a *T.L.O.* standard give discretion to school personnel. Furthermore, their actions must be related to legitimate pedagogical concerns or the reasonable suspicion standard.

Safford v. Redding, 2009

Principals may be faced with searching for lost or stolen devices, and such searches may require the search of individual students. Although the case of *Safford v. Redding* (2009) does not directly apply to technology, the guidelines the decision provides are extremely important for principals to understand should they find themselves faced with searching for a device such as a cell phone. The court placed strict guidelines on strip searches of students, and principals should take note that such searches are considered highly intrusive, and absent some imminent danger, strip-searching a student for an electronic device would be prohibited.

The U.S. Supreme Court has not ruled directly on an education-related case involving the search of cell phone contents, but a case in 2014 may provide guidance, in part due to the forcefulness of the decision. The court ruled unanimously that police could not conduct warrantless searches of cell phones of criminal suspects in custody (*Riley v. California*, 2014). The court concluded that cell phones and other devices were such a major aspect of people's lives that their contents should be considered different from searching occasional items.

THE APPLICATION OF STUDENT RIGHTS AND STUDENT MISUSE OF TECHNOLOGY

The rapid increase in the student use of technology and the unlimited reach of social media has expanded speech issues into uncharted territory for administrators. Well before technology was invented and social media popularized, generations of students have, unfortunately, made threats to others, made fun of their teachers and principals, bullied their classmates, and caused school disruptions with their words or actions.

What new technology has allowed is more rapid and wider dissemination of all of that and more—with the added "advantages" of anonymity, distance, and 24-hour-a-day potential. Principals cannot simply apply "prior restraint" and not allow such messages to ever reach other students and teachers; much of their work must be in the form of prevention or disciplinary action after the fact.

The Important Distinction between On-Campus and Off-Campus Behaviors

The rise of social media gives new meaning to the language in *Tinker* that stated "conduct by the student, in class or out of it, which for any reason—whether it stems from time, place, or type of behavior—materially disrupts class work or involves substantial disorder or invasion of the rights of others" is not protected speech (*Tinker v. Des Moines*, p. 513). "In class or out of it" certainly has a different meaning now from when *Tinker* was decided. Additionally, technology brings new dimensions into the concept of "invasion of the rights of others," leading to the conclusion that it is the message rather than the method of delivery that is important.

Technology changes the nature of the boundaries of the school, but it does not have to confuse or paralyze school officials from taking action when warranted. The key is whether there is a connection, or nexus, between the out-of-school conduct and any school disruption. The courts will consider whether the conduct was related to the school program or if it had a direct impact on school discipline or the safety and welfare of the students and staff. Further, any action the school takes must be reasonable in scope and related to an educational purpose.

Prior to *Tinker*, the courts generally deferred to the judgment of school officials and gave wide latitude to their decisions regarding school discipline. Historically, courts have not been inclined to intervene unless they determined an incident had little or no relationship to the school. Technology blurs the boundaries of what defines on-campus and off-campus behavior, and additionally challenges the nexus between the behavior and the school.

But as far back as 1969, a federal district court in Texas wrote, "[S]chool officials may not judge a student's behavior while he is in his home with his family nor does it seem to this court that they should have jurisdiction over his acts on a public street corner" (*Sullivan v. Houston Indep. Sch. Dist.*,

p. 1340, 1969). This decision implies that the standard should be that it is parental authority, not school authority, that deals with the behavior of a student who is off-campus. When students are off-campus they are best considered citizens, and only on-campus should they be considered students.

However, now technology and social media brings off-campus student behavior to school as could not be imagined in 1969. Principals today may be wise to consider the advice of McCarthy (2014) who states when it comes to the misuse of technology and social media, principals should first consider where the message lands, rather than from where it was launched. Such a focus places the emphasis on the victim or the target, rather than on where the sender of the message was located when the message was sent.

The Application of Student Speech Rights and Social Media and Parody Threats

Students make threats to others through the use of social media, and although there are several considerations that must be taken into account, such as trying to discern the intent of the speaker, courts generally support school disciplinary action for speech that is threatening in nature, whether the targets are students or staff. There is some evidence to conclude courts are more likely to support discipline of students who target classmates than that of those who target staff members, but that is not always the case (McCarthy, 2018).

"True threats" are not protected speech, and when dealing with threatening off-campus speech, courts are supportive of school discipline even in cases where the speech was not a "true threat." School regulation of student speech that disparages or parodies other students is generally given more support than similar speech against staff members.

School authorities under *Tinker* may regulate and punish speech that causes or is likely to cause imminent and substantial disruption or invade the rights of others. The challenges for school administrators as they attempt to keep students safe require them to respond and take action against students who violate laws and policies, to be vigilant regarding student threats and to know about student speech and symbolic speech issues, and to be aware of how cyber threats outside of the school must be dealt with. Principals should keep in mind that they generally may take actions responding to cyber threats in the same manner they handle any other threats or expressions of violence.

School administrators must take threats seriously, regardless if technology was used to make the threat. Language could be considered a threat even if there was no disruption of the school. Upon investigation of potential threats, administrators must consider what constitutes a potential or actual disruption of the school, as well as the intent of the speaker. This is an area where context matters; what is a disruption at one school may not be a disruption at a different school.

When relying on the *Tinker* standard, administrators must also be able to demonstrate there was a high likelihood of imminent disruption or an actual disruption. "[*T*]*inker* does not require school officials to wait until the horse has left the barn before closing the door. . . . [I]t does not require certainty, only that the forecast of substantial disruption be reasonable" (*J.S. v. Blue Mountain Sch. Dist.*, 2011, p. 22, citing *Lowery v. Euverard*, 2007).

What this means in practice is that school administrators don't have to wait until disruptions occur before they take action, but they are also cautioned not to create the actual disruption themselves.

Because of the need to focus on school safety, the courts have sided with school districts in cases of threats delivered off campus via social media. A court in 2015 upheld the suspension of a student who posted a rap song on YouTube and Facebook that was deemed to be harassing and threatening to two coaches. The court in *Bell v. Itawamba County School Board* (2015) found that the rap song was intentionally directed toward the school community and could be reasonably understood to have threatened school staff members.

In *D.J.M. v. Hannibal* (2011) a district court ruled that instant messages sent from a student to classmates referencing plans for a school shooting caused a substantial disruption when administrators had to spend considerable time alleviating the safety concerns of students and stakeholders.

The courts have upheld the disciplining of students who create off-campus threats, even when they could be deemed not true threats. In Pennsylvania, the expulsion of a student was upheld in the case of a website produced off-campus that depicted a teacher with her head cut off and offered $20 to hire a hit man to kill her (*J.S. ex rel. H.S. v Bethlehem Area Sch. Dist.* 2002). Although the court concluded the website was not an actual threat, it viewed the stress on the staff sufficiently disruptive to justify expelling the student.

In another case, school officials were allowed to discipline a student after he sent a message with a crude drawing of a gun firing a bullet into a person's head with blood splattering. Underneath the picture were the words "Kill Mr. VanderMolen." In this case the court held it did not matter if the message constituted a true threat, because it was reasonable for the school to foresee the risk of a substantial disruption (*Wisniewski v. Bd. of Educ.*, 2007).

Cases that did not involve technology but are based on the same legal foundations help to illustrate the issues. In 1998 a student was disciplined after showing his teacher a poem he wrote about loneliness and desperation that ended with shooting twenty-eight people. Upholding the discipline of the student, the court recognized a dilemma between freedom of expression and student safety and noted that in hindsight the school may have overreacted, but emphasized that courts must defer to school officials. "In connection with the safety of their students even when freedom of expression is involved . . . school officials have a difficult task in balancing safety concerns against chilling free expression. This case demonstrates how difficult that task can be" (*LaVine v. Blaine School District,* p. 992, 2001).

In a Texas case, school officials suspended a student after it was learned he had written and shared a journal that discussed creating a neo-Nazi group at school and included plans that included a school shooting (*Ponce v. Socorro,* 2007). Although the student insisted that the account was fictional, the Fifth Circuit Court of Appeals stressed that school officials must take threats such as those in the journal seriously or they may miss signals that lead to tragedy. They must be able "to react quickly and decisively to address a threat of physical violence against their students, without worrying that they will have to face years of litigation second-guessing their judgment as to whether the threat posed a real risk of substantial disturbance" (*Ponce v. Socorro,* p. 772, 2007).

This is a particularly difficult problem when dealing with parodies of staff and students. Several court decisions may discourage principals as they deal with the growing problem. In general, the bar is higher to claim substantial disruption of school that involves parody or disparaging remarks or actions toward a staff member.

In *Klein v. Smith* (1986), a court ruled that Maine school officials went too far disciplining a student for giving the finger to a teacher in a restaurant parking lot. School policy called for disciplinary action for "vulgar or extremely inappropriate language or conduct directed to a staff member" (*Klein v. Smith,* p. 1441). The student was suspended for ten days but a court felt there was no connection between the act in a parking lot far from the school and the operation of the school.

Calvert (2001) properly predicted the future when he stated, "Students create Web sites that give a metaphorical middle finger to teachers and administrators. Just as Jason Klein flipped off a teacher in a parking lot, students today are doing the same in cyberspace" (p. 275). In *Buessink v. Woodland R-IV School District,* a 1998 Missouri court stated school officials violated a student's rights when they suspended him for making a webpage that criticized the principal, teachers, and the school. That the principal was offended by the content of the website was not legal grounds to suppress the speech.

A middle school student created a MySpace profile of her principal that included sexual innuendo and vulgar derogatory comments about both him and his wife. She included comments in the fake profile interests that included "hitting on students and their parents" (*J.S. ex rel. v. Blue Mountain Sch. Dist.* 2011). The school district prevailed at the district court level, but the

Third Circuit Court of Appeals determined that the school's power to limit her speech under *Bethel v. Fraser* did not exist for off-campus speech, and instead should be guided by the *Tinker* test. They determined that there was insufficient disruption of the school to deny her freedom of speech, and that although her writing was "indisputably vulgar" it was so nonsensical that few took it seriously (*J.S. v. Blue Mountain Sch. Dist.*, 2011).

This important case was merged with another Third Circuit case during the appeals process because, while similar in nature, two district courts came to different conclusions (*Layshock ex rel. Layshock v. Hermitage Sch. Dist.*, 2011). Justin Layshock was a seventeen-year-old who used his grandmother's computer to create a fake profile of his principal. The profile stated that the principal was "too drunk to remember" his birthday, along with other crude commentary.

Layshock ultimately prevailed in court when it ruled that there was no nexus between the speech and any substantial disruption of the school, a conclusion that was not challenged by the school on appeal. The court concluded that he should not be punished merely because his speech reached the school, and the court did not wish to set a precedent giving school officials the same authority off campus as they would have on campus.

> Allowing the District to punish Justin for conduct he engaged in while at his grandmother's house using his grandmother's computer would create just such a precedent, and we therefore conclude that the district court correctly ruled that the District's response to Justin's expressive conduct violated the First Amendment guarantee of free expression. (*Layshock v. Hermitage* p. 217, 2011)

In 2011, the full Third Circuit reviewed both cases and ruled in favor of both students, holding that schools are prevented from reaching beyond the school to impose discipline that may otherwise be appropriate had the infraction occurred inside of the school. The U.S. Supreme Court denied the merged cases on appeals by the school districts, leaving the issue for schools somewhat unsettled (*Blue Mountain v. J.S. ex rel. Snyder,* 2012).

There are other circumstances that contribute to the dilemma faced by principals. In *J.C. v. Beverly Hills* (2010) the action of the school was not supported when a student was disciplined for posting a YouTube video that directed insults and profanity against a particular student. The video was created and posted off campus. Although the victim felt "humiliation," there was no indication that the video was viewed on campus computers and there was insufficient evidence of a disruption of the school. Students merely talking about seeing contents of a website is not enough of a threshold to reach the level of a substantial disruption.

A student in Florida created a Facebook group for other students to post their dislike of a teacher. The student posted, "Ms. Sarah Phelps is the worst teacher I've ever met! To those select students who have had the displeasure of having Ms. Sarah Phelps, or simply knowing her and her insane antics: Here is the place to express your feelings of hatred" (*Evans v. Bayer*, p. 1367, 2010).

The student prevailed in court after she challenged the suspension given to her by her principal. The court held that the website "was an opinion of a student about a teacher, that was published off-campus, did not cause any disruption on-campus, and was not lewd, vulgar, threatening, or advocating illegal or dangerous behavior" (*Evans v. Bayer,* p. 1374, 2010).

Not all students have prevailed in court after being disciplined for off-campus speech.

After a student was upset with an administrative decision, she posted messages on her home computer criticizing the "douchebags in the central office" (*Doninger v. Niehoff,* 2011). She also urged students to take action to "piss them off more" and was disciplined by the school. The court ruled that there was enough evidence to support a reasonable forecast of disruption of the school. When brothers created a parody website with racially and sexually offensive comments directed at students, school officials were allowed to discipline the students for the disruption it caused (*S.J.W. v. Lee's Summit R-7 Sch. Dist.,* 2012).

School discipline was upheld in a case where a student created a MySpace page called S.A.S.H. that was claimed to mean "Students Against Sluts Herpes" (*Kowalski v. Berkeley County Schools*, 2011). The page was largely created to target a particular student, and testimony indicated the acronym actually meant "Students Against Shays Herpes," the student who was the primary discussion topic of the page. The court held that the school was justified in their punishment because the student used the internet to orchestrate an attack on a classmate and it was connected enough to the school to allow them to regulate the speech under *Tinker*. The student "may have pushed her computer's keys at home but she knew that the electronic response would be . . . published beyond her home . . . and could reasonably be expected to reach the school or impact the school environment" (*Kowalski v. Berkeley,* p. 573, 2011).

Principals must make decisions related to their responses to social media parody, and must also consider when such parody crosses the line into harassment and bullying. Even when considering the potential negative effects of social media and parody of staff, students should also have some form of conditional privilege to comment on or criticize school officials or practices. The difficulty may be how to determine if such commentary crosses an established (and often moving) line.

EDUCATIONAL LAW ISSUES: (3) STUDENT BULLYING, HARASSMENT, AND THREATS

The problem of student harassment and bullying (through any means, including social media) requires action by school principals. School districts that fail to appropriately identify, thwart, and remedy harassment and bullying risk violating federal civil rights laws. In cases of threats, bullying, or harassment, school officials are not only morally obligated to take action, but in many instances legally mandated to respond.

Schools are responsible for addressing harassment and bullying about which it knows or reasonably should have known. In October 2010, the U.S. Department of Education Office of Civil Rights (OCR) issued a "Dear Colleague" letter addressing bullying and harassment in schools. It made clear that the OCR has authority to enforce Section 504 of the Rehabilitation Act and Title II of the Americans with Disabilities Act. State and federal antibullying laws and their resulting policies require principals to address this problem.

With respect to bullying and harassment through social media, principals are obligated to take appropriate action when faced with such incidences. In most cases, such bullying is described as repeated occurrences that result in physical or emotional harm, places a person in reasonable fear, creates a hostile environment, impinges on the rights of others, or materially and substantially disrupts the operation of the school (Sneed, 2013).

Cyberbullying is difficult to monitor and is among the fastest growing types of bullying. Surveys report that up to 43 percent of teens report being victims, and such victims are more than twice as likely to have attempted suicide compared to youths who have not been cyberbullied (Sneed, 2013).

School principals should be aware of district policies regarding bullying and harassment, whether technology is involved or not, and need to investigate and take disciplinary action based on the facts. The law in the area of cyberbullying is evolving, but the foundations set forth in *Tinker* and *Fraser* still apply. In general, cyberbullying and harassment should be addressed in school policy and student handbooks, and students should be educated about the expectations of the school. Creating a supportive school climate is the most important step in preventing bullying and harassment (Sneed, 2013). It is also important to train all staff to recognize sexting, bullying, and harassment problems, and to protect victims who come forward with information.

EDUCATIONAL LAW ISSUES: (4) SEXTING

One form of harassment and bullying that may involve technology is what has become known as "sexting," the sending of nude or seminude pictures via social media. The issue is one that centers around internet safety, in general, and schools are obligated to educate students about the dangers of sexting. Not all sexting incidences involve bullying and harassment, because acts of sexting may be consensual. However, sexting is a problem even when it does not involve bullying or harassment (Hachiya, 2017).

Early efforts to confront sexting issues demonstrate the difficulty in addressing it. In one case, school officials learned of seminude photos being circulated on cell phones, and they eventually found and sent the photos to the local district attorney. The district attorney chose to offer the nineteen girls involved a deal to either take a required "reeducation program" designed around the "responsibilities of being a girl" or face prosecution for possession of child pornography. Sixteen of the girls chose to take the class, but others filed suit. Ultimately, in *Miller v. Skumanick* (2009) the students did not face prosecution.

In another sexting case, students posted photographs on social media they took during several sleepovers that showed girls sucking on phallic-shaped lollipops, as well as clothed photos of themselves in provocative positions and imitating sex acts (*T.V. ex rel. B.V. v. Smith-Green Cmty. Sch.,* 2011). In testimony the girls said they posted them to be funny and that they were only joking around. The images came to light after parents of uninvolved students brought them to school officials.

The girls were subsequently prohibited from being members of their volleyball team because the school determined there was a disruption of the school, and that the girls had violated the student handbook that stated, "[I]f you act in a manner in school or out of school that brings discredit or dishonor upon yourself or your school, you may be removed from extra-curricular activities for all or part of the year" (*T.V. ex rel. B.V. v. Smith-Green,* p. 773, 2011).

The students ultimately prevailed in court as the judge concluded that there was no real disruption of the school other than disagreement among the team, and that the photos were not lewd or vulgar. In addition, the judge stated the school handbook policy related to off-campus behavior was vague and overbroad.

For principals, sexting is a serious issue that creates an intersection between possible criminal charges, sexual harassment and bullying concerns, and Fourth Amendment search issues, which are addressed in the next section. If sexting is discovered, keep in mind local mandatory-reporting laws and involve parents and law enforcement if necessary.

THE APPLICATION OF STUDENT RIGHTS RELATED TO SEARCHES OF ELECTRONIC DEVICES AND MONITORING OF STUDENT SOCIAL MEDIA

Absent sufficient reasons to search the contents of an electronic device, principals should avoid searching it, but if they make the decision to search a device, they should define the scope of their search. A student's mere possession of a device does not make for a reasonable cause to search it.

The decision to conduct a technology-related search of a student is guided by the standards set forth in the *T.L.O.* decision. There are differences between searching *for* a device and searching *the contents* of a device. The search must be justified at inception—when the search begins, and reasonable in scope—how far and extensive the search becomes. The search by school police would require the higher standard of probable cause.

Strip-searching a student for an electronic device would be guided by *Safford v. Redding*, and absent some form of imminent danger to the student or others, the search would likely be prohibited for school officials. For law enforcement to conduct such a search, probable cause would be required.

School computers and devices checked out to students present a different expectation of student privacy. School districts should have policy and language in student handbooks that states computers and devices are subject to search when there is reasonable suspicion that a search of the device will reveal that school policy has been violated. The understanding of a limited expectation of student privacy would be similar to that expected with the use of school lockers.

Sound principal discretion is advised when making the decision to search electronic devices. There may be situations where searching a device is reasonable based on information provided by a student. For example, a student may show a principal text messages that may create a reasonable circumstance to search the device of another student. Other examples include a student showing school officials messages that are inappropriate or pose imminent danger and there is information about where the messages originated. Caution is advised to limit the search, however, to the inappropriate messages.

There are common situations where searching an electronic device is likely unjustified and unreasonable. Stopping a student in the hallway who is talking on a cell phone is not justification in itself to conduct a search of a phone. Attempting to "prove" that a student was using a device in violation of school policy might also be considered unjustified, or considered unreasonable if the scope of the search went beyond checking to see if the device was recently used. For example, it would not be reasonable to search the photographs stored in a device merely because a student arrived to class late or was seen using the device in class.

Extreme caution is advised when principals gain information about a device that may include images of child pornography, and in those situations, principals should cease their search and immediately turn to law enforcement. For their own protection, under no circumstances should principals control or possess a device known to contain child pornography other than to give the device to law enforcement.

Some examples of searches that may *not* be justified or reasonable include:

- Searching a student cell phone contact list and contacting students for the purpose of finding potential cell phone violators when they respond (*Klump v. Nazareth,* 2006)
- Searching the contents of a cell phone of a student accused of possessing drugs after patting down the student and searching other possessions (*Gallimore v. Henrico,* 2014) because unlike the other possessions, "the cell phone could not have contained drugs"
- "Extending the walls of the schoolhouse" under the standards of *T.L.O.* by school officials attempting to search computers at the home of a student (*Ianson v. Zion-Benton,* 2001)

While school officials may search contents of school-issued devices, without reasonable suspicion they must take caution searching private student accounts and password-protected accounts without permission. Searching a student device without the student's knowledge or permission after gaining knowledge of their passwords led to a monetary settlement in a Minnesota School District (*R.S. v. Minnewaska,* 2012).

SUGGESTIONS FOR POLICY AND PRACTICE RELATED TO STUDENTS AND TECHNOLOGY

As new technologies emerge, schools should adapt their policies from "acceptable use" to "responsible use" in order to educate students about proper and safe behavior across all technology platforms. Acceptable use policies tend to become lists of prohibited actions that are almost out of date as soon as they are published and can never be inclusive of every possible misuse of technology by a student. Responsible use policies, on the other hand, should be geared toward teaching students, in an age-appropriate manner, how to be safe, respectful, and legal while using all forms of technology.

Considerations Related to Off-Campus-Generated Social Media Messages

- Did the student send the message directly to members of the school community?
- Did the student post on a site that is available to the general public or members of the school community?
- Did the student discuss, access, or encourage others to access the message while at school?
- Did the student use school-provided technology and/or violate usage policy?

Considerations Related to Matters of Threatening Speech

- Courts strongly support school disciplinary action for threats against students and staff.
- Speech does not need to be a "true threat" in order for courts to support school discipline.
- It is often wise to involve law enforcement.

Considerations Related to Speech That Disparages Staff

- Most of the time it does not meet the test of material or substantial disruption.
- Consider the degree to which the speech was seen—widely or limited?
- Consider the degree to which the content was/could be accessed by students while at school.

Considerations Related to Speech that Disparages/Bullies/Harasses Students

- Courts have generally supported action against students who disparage other students.
- Follow state law and district policy related to bullying and harassment.
- Consider how widely the speech was accessed by students at school.
- Carefully consider the impact of the speech on the victim—for example, on his or her school performance and participation, problems with peers, increased anxiety.
- Consider if the speech inspired others to conduct similar behavior.
- Determine if the speech has incited other types of confrontations.

Considerations Regarding Policy Issues and Student Handbooks

- Address issues on an age-appropriate basis.
- Address problems from an educational perspective first, and a punitive standpoint second.
- The establishment of an open climate of communication increases the overall school safety environment.
- Develop and widely publicize responsible-use policies that include examples of acceptable activities and unacceptable activities. Teach the digital citizenship and responsible-use policies outlined in the handbook. Include in the handbook the topics of cyber safety, antibullying, and anti-harassment and teach what they mean in an age-appropriate manner.
- Have clear language in school policy stating that outside of school, behavior (especially through the use of social media) may be subject to discipline if it involves bullying and harassment of any kind, toward students or staff, or if the behavior disrupts the school.
- Ensure that policies focus on the impact of the expression and not the content.
- Specifically address a limited expectation of privacy for school-issued devices and platforms.
- Specifically address your authority to regulate and monitor the use of school-issued devices and platforms.
- Create separate policies for students and for staff.
- In an age-appropriate manner, enlist students in your cyber safety and antibullying efforts.
- Think about unintended consequences if you consider monitoring teacher and student use of social media.
- Tread carefully when considering any use of student-tracking devices; adhere to state and local laws.

CONCLUSION

Education law related to technology issues in schools is an emerging and unsettled area of school law. When dealing with problems associated with misuse of technology, principals can rely on their basic foundational knowledge of student rights and their own obligations and responsibilities to maintain a safe and orderly environment. Even though new technology can create changes faster than principals sometimes think they can keep pace, the truth is there should be no problems associated with technology that outweigh the benefits advanced technology can bring to students, staff, and schools.

REFERENCES

AJC. (2010). Barrow teacher fired over Facebook still not back in classroom. Retrieved from http://www.ajc.com/news/news/local/barrow-teacher-fired-over-facebook-still-not-back-/nQmpS/#_federated=1.

Bathon, J. M., & Brady, K. P. (2010). Teacher free speech and expression in a digital age: A legal analysis. National Association of Secondary School Principals. *NASSP Bulletin, 94*(3), 213–226. Retrieved from http://search.proquest.com.er.lib.k-state.edu/docview/853644048?accountid=11789.

Bell v. Itawamba School Board, 782 F.3d 712 (5th Cir. 2015).

Bethel School Dist. No. 403 v. Fraser, 478 U.S. 675, 106 S. Ct. 3159, 92 L. Ed. 2d 549 (1986).

Blue Mountain School District v. J.S., 132 S. Ct. 1097, 181 L. Ed. 2d 978 (2012).

Buessink v. Woodland R-IV Sch. Dist., 30 F.Supp.2d 1175 (E.D. Mo. 1998).

Calvert, C. (2001). Off-campus speech, on-campus punishment: Censorship of the emerging Internet underground. *Boston University Journal of Science & Technology Law, 7*, pp. 243–271.

D.J.M. v. Hannibal Public School Dist. No. 60, 647 F.3d 754 (8th Cir. 2011).

Doninger v. Niehoff, 642 F.3d 334 (2d Cir. 2011).

Evans v. Bayer, 684 F. Supp. 2d 1365 (S.D. Fla. 2010).

Gallimore v. Henrico County School Board, Civil Case No. 3: 14cv00009 (E.D. Va. Aug. 5, 2014).

Gallman, S. (2015). Texas teacher fired after Ferguson tweets. *CNN*. Retrieved March 24, 2015, from http://www.cnn.com/2014/11/14/us/texas-teacher-fired-ferguson-tweet/index.html?hpt=hp_t2.

Garcetti v. Ceballos, 547 U.S. 410, 126 S. Ct. 1951, 164 L. Ed. 2d 689 (2006).

Hachiya, Robert F. (2017). Dangers for principals and students when conducting investigations of sexting in schools. *Clearing House: A Journal of Educational Strategies, Issues and Ideas, 90*(5–6), p. 177–183.

Hazelwood School Dist. v. Kuhlmeier, 484 U.S. 260, 108 S. Ct. 562, 98 L. Ed. 2d 592 (1988).

Helms, A. (2008). Charlotte teachers face actions because of Facebook postings. *The Charlotte Observer*. Retrieved from http://www.heraldonline.com/news/local/article12241319.html.

Ianson v. Zion-Benton Township High School, 2001 WL 18521 (N.D. Ill).

Imber, M., Van Geel, T., Blokhuis, J., & Feldman, J. (2014). *A teacher's guide to education law* (5th ed.). New York City: Routledge.

J.C. ex rel. R.C. v. Beverly Hills Unified School, 711 F. Supp. 2d 1094 (C.D. Cal. 2010).

J.S. ex rel. H.S. v Bethlehem Area Sch. Dist., 807 A.2d 847 (Pa. 2002).

J.S. ex rel. Snyder v. Blue Mountain School Dist., 650 F.3d 915 (3d Cir. 2011).

Klein v. Smith, 635 F.Supp.1440 (D. Me 1986).

Klump v. Nazareth Area School District, 425 F.Supp.2d 622 (E.D. Pa. 2006).

Kowalski v. Berkeley County Schools, 652 F.3d 565 (4th Cir. 2011).

LaVine v. Blaine School District., 257 F.3d 981 (9th Cir. 2001).

Layshock ex rel. Layshock v. Hermitage School Dist., 650 F.3d 205 (3d Cir. 2011).
Lowery v. Euverard, 497 F.3d 584 (6th Cir. 2007).
McCarthy, M. (2014). Tinkering with student speech: Emerging legal debates in P-20 education. Symposium at the American Educational Research Association Annual Meeting, Philadelphia, April 2014.
McCarthy, M. (2018). Off-campus sexually harassing expression: What legal standard applies? *Brigham Young University Education and Law Journal*, 2018, (1), 22.
Miller v. Skumanick, 605 F. Supp. 2d 634 (M.D. Pa. 2009).
Morse v. Frederick, 127 S. Ct. 2618, 551 U.S. 393, 168 L. Ed. 2d 290 (2007).
Mt. Healthy City Bd. of Ed. v. Doyle, 429 U.S. 274, 97 S. Ct. 568, 50 L. Ed. 2d 471 (1977).
New Jersey v. T.L.O., 469 U.S. 325, 105 S. Ct. 733, 83 L. Ed. 2d 720 (1985).
Newman, A. (2013). Brooklyn teacher who talked out of school can keep her job. *New York Times*, May 9. Retrieved from http://www.nytimes.com/2013/05/09/nyregion/brooklyn-teacher-who-talked-out-of-school-can-keep-her-job.html?_r=1.
Pickering v. Board of Ed. of Township High School Dist. 205, Will Cty., 391 U.S. 563, 88 S. Ct. 1731, 20 L. Ed. 2d 811 (1968).
Ponce v. Socorro, 508 F.3d 765 (5th Cir. 2007).
Riley v. California, 134 S. Ct. 2473, 573 U.S., 189 L. Ed. 2d 430 (2014).
R.S. v. Minnewaska Area Sch. Distr. No 2149., 894 F.Supp.2d 1128 (D. Minn., 2012).
Safford Unified School Dist. No. 1 v. Redding, 129 S. Ct. 2633, 557 U.S. 364, 174 L. Ed. 2d 354 (2009).
Simpson, M. (2015). Social networking nightmares. *NEA*. Retrieved March 26, 2015, from http://www.nea.org/home/38324.htm.
S.J.W. ex rel. Wilson v. Lee's Summit School Dist., 696 F.3d 771 (8th Cir. 2012).
Sneed, M. (2013). Bullying, cyberbullying and harassment: What school districts need to know to protect their students and themselves. Lecture, Columbia Law School: School Law Institute.
Snyder v. Millersville University, Civil Action. No. 07–1660 (E.D. Pa. Dec. 3, 2008).
Spanierman v. Hughes, 576 F. Supp. 2d 292 (D. Conn. 2008).
Stoss, R. (2007). How to lose your job on your own time, *New York Times*, Dec. 30. Retrieved from http://www.nytimes.com/2007/12/30/business/30digi.html.
Sullivan v. Houston Indep. Sch. Dist., 307 F.Supp.1328 (S.D. Tex. 1969).
Tinker v. Des Moines Independent Community School Dist., 393 U.S. 503, 89 S. Ct. 733, 21 L. Ed. 2d 731 (1969).
T.V. ex rel. B.V. v. Smith-Green Community School, 807 F. Supp. 2d 767 (N.D. Ind. 2011).
Walsh, M. (2014). Teacher's blog posts slamming students not protected, judge rules. *Education Week: The School Law Blog*, July 31. Retrieved March 10, 2015, from http://blogs.edweek.org/edweek/school_law/2014/07/teachers_blog_posts_slamming_s.html?utm_source=feedblitz&utm_medium=FeedBlitzRss&utm_campaign=theschoollawblog.
Wisniewski v. Bd. of Educ., 494 F3d. 34 (2nd Cir. 2007).

Chapter Five

Using a Spreadsheet Pivot Table to Do an Equity Audit for Social Justice

Dana Christman and Gary Ivory

KEY POINTS IN THIS CHAPTER

- We review social justice perspectives on education and leadership.
- We review the place of equity audits in pursuing social justice in schools.
- We discuss how percentages serve well to compare groups to one another and offer cautions about how to use them appropriately.
- We illustrate with fictitious data how Excel's pivot table function can be used to compare groups of students on their participation in school programs.
- Finally, we recommend steps to engage members of the school community in reflecting on findings from an equity audit and moving from reflection to action.

You may know that spreadsheet programs can support decision making. Particularly with regard to developing a budget, spreadsheets are wonderful, as they allow you to lay out the items and costs, create formulas to calculate the bottom line, and then try out different scenarios to see the effect on that bottom line. We discuss in this chapter another useful application: using the pivot table application in a spreadsheet to monitor which of your school programs serve all groups of students equitably. This is one component of an equity audit (Scheurich & Skrla, 2003; Skrla et al., 2004, 2010). We see the equity audit as a tool to bring about social justice.

SOCIAL JUSTICE, EQUITY, AND SOCIAL JUSTICE LEADERSHIP

People differ on what social justice means. So let us look to the scholarly literature for some help. For example, Gewirtz (1998) indicates that social justice must interrupt and disengage from actions that tend to isolate and silence underrepresented groups and individuals. Goldfarb and Grinberg (2002) define social justice "as the exercise of altering these [institutional and organizational] arrangements by actively engaging in reclaiming, appropriating, sustaining, and advancing inherent human rights of equity, equality, and fairness in social, economic, educational, and personal dimensions" (p. 162). Aligning equity with social justice practice, Gorski (2013) postulates that equity represents a "commitment to fairness, to equal opportunity, to fair distribution of resources" (p. 20). Similarly, Green (2017) states his definition of equity as "fair access to and distribution of opportunities, power, and resources, within and outside of schools that can improve children's life outcomes" (p. 6). As Furman (2012) points out, "A common understanding among many leadership scholars is that social justice focuses on the experiences of marginalized groups and inequities in educational opportunities and outcomes" (p. 194).

Skrla, McKenzie, and Scheurich (2009) sum it up well. They write that social justice in education would mean that "[e]very learner—in whatever learning environment that learner is found—has the greatest opportunity to learn, enhanced by the supports necessary to achieve competence, excellence, independence, responsibility, and self-sufficiency for school and for life" (p. 14).

Practicing social justice in schools, then, manifests as a deliberative action; social justice does not happen without intention. To move toward equity among all students, educational leaders must make purposeful efforts to ensure that schools are welcoming places for all students and their communities. In the bigger picture, educational leaders must also heed calls from the state and media demanding accountability in schools. As Blackmore (2009) explains, "The state is no longer able to ignore issues of educational inequality" (p. 8).

Unfortunately, social justice also does not happen without resistance. So what falls to educational leaders is a commitment to leading with social justice. Such commitment must not only be espoused, but must be upheld with unwavering conviction and action. There is often much resistance from teachers, administrators, and even the communities in which the school resides, and from other stakeholders as well. School leaders must act as catalysts in shaping the structures and cultures of schools in the change process (McKenzie et al., 2008; Scanlan, 2013; Theoharis, 2007).

Principals, teachers, and other administrators must be willing to learn new skills and acquire new knowledge. Furman (2012) suggests that educational leaders think of their leadership as praxis, that is, involving both reflection and practice. She indicates that

> Praxis involves the continual, dynamic interaction among knowledge acquisition, deep reflection, and action at two levels—the intrapersonal and the extrapersonal—with the purpose of transformation and liberation. At the intrapersonal level, praxis involves self-knowledge, critical self-reflection, and acting to transform oneself as a leader for social justice. At the extrapersonal level, praxis involves knowing and understanding systemic social justice issues, reflecting on these issues, and taking action to address them. (p. 203)

Social justice leaders also must be transformative. They must "develop a heightened and critical awareness of oppression, exclusion, and marginalization" (Brooks & Miles, 2006, p. 5). Thus, we note that social justice leaders must be deliberate, intentional, accountable, and reflective, as well as willing to take risks, learn new skills, and create a culture of change. This is the essence of the social justice leader in transforming schools.

EQUITY AUDITS

Now, let us move to practical steps. One of the first actions we can take is doing an equity audit. Social justice leaders need tools to assess their schools for equity and inclusion. Conducting equity audits is one way to tackle the issue of equity in schools. Equity audits are a systematic way for school leaders and others to assess and analyze the level of equity or inequity present in their schools or districts (Scheurich & Skrla, 2003; Skrla et al., 2004, 2010).

> In its most pure form, an equity audit is a data collection activity that spans all areas/facets of a school or district environment. Participants analyze the body of data collected to identify areas for improvement (in the most unbiased way possible). When multiple weaknesses are identified, participants must prioritize and make decisions (based on personal ethics, school/district goals, available resources, etc.) about which areas to target for improvement plans. (University Council for Educational Administration, 2014, para. 1)

There are several elements in almost all equity audits in education (Green, 2017). For example, Skrla et al. (2004) and Skrla, McKenzie, and Scheurich (2009) provide an equity audit process that investigates twelve markers across three categories: teacher quality equity, programmatic equity, and achievement equity.

These researchers propose an implementation process with seven steps: (1) create a committee of relevant stakeholders, (2) present the data to the stakeholders and enlist them in graphing the data, (3) discuss the meaning of the data, (4) discuss potential solutions, (5) implement solutions, (6) monitor and evaluate results, and (7) celebrate successes and/or return to step 3 of the process.

We suggest that readers use the equity audit process that Skrla, McKenzie, and Scheurich (2009) recommend. The path to equity is complex, messy, and grounded in the local context. Each school and community is unique. The strength of the audit lies in the process of looking at your specific conditions and addressing them with your specific strengths. We will come back to the steps in the process toward the end of this chapter. For now, for just an example, let us use the Excel pivot table to analyze some data.

USING PERCENTAGES

We begin here with some basic thoughts about percentages. After those thoughts, we will use Excel's pivot tables to calculate percentages that will show whether a school program is serving a particular group of students equitably. Then, we will return to Skrla, McKenzie, and Scheurich's (2009) steps in an equity audit.

We realize some readers learned how to calculate percentages in elementary or middle school and have understood them well ever since. Those readers may be bored to death by this next section. But we have also seen people, some of them quite competent leaders, who have a weak grasp of percentages. So we offer a couple pages of refresher here. If you already have a handle on percentages, feel free to skip this section.

Percentages provide a way to compare the rates at which things happen. Imagine a fellow educator at a cocktail party telling you about his or her high school in these words:

> We're very proud of our students this year because two hundred of them got college scholarships. That's way more than our neighbor school (Eastern United HS) did. Of course, Eastern United had two hundred fewer seniors than we did. Our football team did really well this year as well. They won eight out of their twelve games, two more than the team from Eastern United. And Eastern United played three more games than our team did.
>
> Another great accomplishment was that six of our teachers earned master's degrees, four of the men and two of the women, but we have ten more women than men as teachers. Eastern United teachers earned only seven master's degrees, but, as I said, they are a smaller school. Three of their master's degrees

went to men and four to women. And they have more men than women as teachers. We tend to be really competitive with Eastern United. I think we really beat them this year.

Is your head spinning by now? If this conversation happened at an actual mixer, would you find yourself fumbling for excuses to slip away? One of the confusing aspects of this conversation was that the high schools seemed to be of different sizes and had different population mixes, so it was difficult to make much sense of the numbers the speaker was tossing out. Here is where percentages come in. Calculating percentages allows us to make fair and simple comparisons among different-sized populations by calculating rates or proportions and comparing them, rather than raw numbers. So, for example, as percentages, the speaker's football comparison would look like table 5.1.

Notice how much easier it is to mentally process the two percentages (we won 66.7 percent of our games; they won only 40 percent of theirs) than the hodge-podge of numbers the speaker threw out at you. You simply divide the number of games won by the number of games played and multiply the quotient by a hundred. Percentages are wonderful in this way. If we want to know if our music programs are serving members of different demographic groups equitably, for example, we can calculate percentages of each demographic group that are participating and make a simple comparison. The same is true for our athletic programs, our ROTC programs, or any of our student clubs.

But you must know which number to divide by which other number, for each of the groups that you want to compare. This can be tricky, especially when you are having a hectic day and people are asking you to attend to other events and issues. We think that is partly why some of us do not remember very well how to use percentages; we have too many distractions to be able to recall how percentages work.

The key here is that we must use analogous numbers in each cell of our table. Once we can do that, it is simple to use an Excel pivot table to do the calculations for us. What do we mean by "analogous"? Simply that we must use comparable numbers for each group. Notice that in table 5.1, row A gives comparable numbers for each school: number of games won. And row B

Table 5.1. Computing Percentages for Games Won

	Speaker's High School	Eastern United High School
Row A: Number of Games Won	8	6
Row B. Total Number of Games Played	12	15
Percent of Games Won	66.7%	40%

gives comparable numbers for each school: number of games played. This is key. If we make sure our raw numbers in the two rows are comparable, then we are on the right track (table 5.2).

Notice that the top numbers are comparable in the two columns (number of games won) and the bottom numbers are comparable (number of games played). Notice further (this can get tricky) that the relationships between the top and bottom numbers are the same in each column, that is, the number of games won is a subset of the total number of games played.

Now contrast that with an error made recently by a government official in a large city. The city newspaper had done a study of racial profiling and reported that after stopping drivers for suspected traffic infractions, the police were more likely to search African Americans than members of other races. In fact, 19 percent of African American drivers who were stopped were then searched. After reading the report, the city official complained, "It can't be that much [19%], because if it is then we have a problem. The demographics of [this city] show we only have 3% African Americans [here]."

It sounds like the city council member was comparing the 19 percent of African Americans who were searched after being stopped to the 3 percent of the city that was African American. This is an example of not using analogous or comparable numbers. Table 5.3 shows a chart of her claim.

The top numbers in each column are not comparable, and the bottom numbers in each column are not comparable. Furthermore, the relationships between the top and bottom numbers are not the same. (Note that the left-hand column compares African American drivers searched to African American drivers stopped; but the second column compares African American people

Table 5.2. Dividing Numbers to Get Percentages

The Speaker's High School	Eastern United High School
Divide number of games won (8) by number of games played (12). Multiply quotient by 100 = 66.7%.	Divide number of games won (6) by number of games played (15). Multiply quotient by 100 = 40%.

Table 5.3. Dividing Numbers to Get the City Councilwoman's Percentages

Divide number of African American drivers searched after being stopped by total number of African American drivers stopped. Multiply by 100 = 19%.	Divide number of African American people living in the city by total number of people living in the city. Multiply by 100 = 3%.

in the city to total number of people living in the city, African Americans and others.)

Notice that just as our football example in table 5.2 has number of games in the top and bottom of both columns, table 5.3 has African American drivers in both the top and bottom of the column on the left. But the column on the right has number of African American people on the top and total number of people in the bottom. That is why we say the two columns are not comparable.

Therefore, the percentages are not comparable. There is absolutely nothing to be learned by comparing the 19 percent to the 3 percent. But as we said, it is easy for busy leaders to make mistakes like this when we have to attend to many different concerns, all at the same time. Furthermore, for purposes of thinking about equity, either column may be a perfectly legitimate way to calculate a percent. But in the city official's comment, the two percentages were just not comparable.

THE EXCEL PIVOT TABLE

Now, let us see how we can use Excel to do an equity audit on a database of students in our school. Suppose that our question was whether our music programs attracted comparable numbers of student participants from each of different groups. When we ask a question like this, we are concerning ourselves with equity. We are justifying our programs based on *the educational opportunities they provide to all groups of students.*

That is, in an equity audit, we do not justify our music program by the fact that we have *always* had a marching band; or that our stage band wins contests every year; or our orchestra program succeeds because so many high-quality stringed instruments have been donated to us; or our band performs at half time of the football games just as *all the other schools' bands* perform at half time.

Any of these may be legitimate reasons for the decisions you make about your music programs. But to be concerned about equity, we must consider the reason we cited above, whether "[e]very learner—in whatever learning environment that learner is found—has the greatest opportunity to learn, enhanced by the supports necessary to achieve competence, excellence, independence, responsibility, and self-sufficiency for school and for life" (Skrla, McKenzie, & Scheurich, 2009, p. 14).

So we might ask the question, do we have music programs that attract students from different groups: ethnic majority and minority, low-income and more affluent, boys and girls, lesbian-gay-bisexual-transgender-queer/questioning-other (LGBTQ+) and straight, and so on? That is a big question, and no statistical analysis can answer it unequivocally for us. We can use percentages, though, to give us clues as to whether we are doing okay in this regard or whether we need to reconsider our usual ways of doing things.

THE ANALYSIS

We suspect that you already have a computerized list of students, and that it already has in it some of the data about students to which you want to attend: for example, their race or ethnicity, their sex, and some indicator of socioeconomic status, as well as other indicators of academic situations.

If you import the computerized list into an electronic spreadsheet such as Excel, you can add information that your district does not normally keep in the student database. If you do not know how to get your student records into a spreadsheet program, you will have to ask a technologically adept person to help you. We will show you just the first twenty records here to illustrate the database. When we illustrate an analysis, we will use a fictional school with an enrollment of 869 students.

Assume the records are already in Excel. Figure 5.1 shows how they will look. Figure 5.1 shows the student records in Excel with four demographic characteristics that often occur to educators when they consider whether their programs are serving all students equitably: sex, ethnicity, lunch program (which indicates a student's economic status), and whether the student is an English Learner.

Suppose, for example, you wanted to know if your school's music program was attractive to students from different groups. You could make an additional column in Excel (column G) for the music program in which each student participated. To keep it simple, we restrict our example to only three choices: band, choir, or none.

In this case, however, we are not really interested in *which* music program students join, but only whether they are in *some* school music program. We will make one more column (column H) with only two possible choices: YES (they participate in a music program, either band or choir) or NO (they do not). Now the records in our database will look like figure 5.2.

Now, let us consider our students who are English Learners. We know it is easy for them to get marginalized due to their lack of familiarity with English; we see their integration into the school community as likely to promote their acquisition of English; and we see participation in music as one among many ways for them to be integrated in the school community and enjoy the sense of belonging and fulfillment we have seen in other music students.

	A	B	C	D	E	F
1	LASTNAME	FIRSTNAME	SEX	ETHNICITY	LUNCH	ENGLISH LEARNER
2	ACOSTA	ABEL	M	Hispanic	Free lunch	No
3	ALBA	JAVIER M	M	Hispanic	Free lunch	No
4	BAEZ	MATTHEW	M	Hispanic	Free lunch	No
5	BATES	CHARLENE A	F	American Indian	Free lunch	No
6	BRADLEY	ALETHEA	F	African American	Free lunch	No
7	CARRIZAL	MONICA	F	Hispanic	Free lunch	No
8	CRAWFORD	BERNADETTE	F	Hispanic	Free lunch	No
9	DEXTER	ABIGAIL	F	White not Hispanic	Free lunch	No
10	DIAZ	ARTURO	M	Hispanic	Free lunch	No
11	ELIZONDO	ANDREA	F	Hispanic	Free lunch	Yes
12	ESCAJEDA	BRENDA	F	Hispanic	Free lunch	No
13	FRAIRE	ABRAHAM	M	Hispanic	Free lunch	No
14	FROST	CHARLES	M	White not Hispanic	Not low income	No
15	GOMEZ	ADRIAN	M	Hispanic	Free lunch	Yes
16	GREENE	BRAD	M	White not Hispanic	Not low income	No
17	HAMILTON	AMBER M	F	White not Hispanic	Free lunch	No
18	HERNANDES	MIGUEL	M	Hispanic	Not low income	No
19	IRIGOYEN	ANTONIO	M	Hispanic	Not low income	No
20	IRIGOYEN	DANIEL	M	Hispanic	Free lunch	Yes
21	JARAMILLO	EVE S	F	Hispanic	Free lunch	No

Figure 5.1. First twenty records in student database

	A	B	C	D	E	F	G	H
1	LASTNAME	FIRSTNAME	SEX	ETHNICITY	LUNCH	ENGLISH LEARNER	MUSIC PROGRAM	MUSIC PARTICIPATION
2	ACOSTA	ABEL	M	Hispanic	Free lunch	No	band	Yes
3	ALBA	JAVIER M	M	Hispanic	Free lunch	No	none	No
4	BAEZ	MATTHEW	M	Hispanic	Free lunch	No	choir	Yes
5	BATES	CHARLENE A	F	American Indian	Free lunch	No	none	No
6	BRADLEY	ALETHEA	F	African American	Free lunch	No	band	Yes
7	CARRIZAL	MONICA	F	Hispanic	Free lunch	No	choir	Yes
8	CRAWFORD	BERNADETTE	F	Hispanic	Free lunch	No	none	No
9	DEXTER	ABIGAIL	F	White not Hispanic	Free lunch	No	none	No
10	DIAZ	ARTURO	M	Hispanic	Free lunch	No	band	Yes
11	ELIZONDO	ANDREA	F	Hispanic	Free lunch	Yes	band	Yes
12	ESCAJEDA	BRENDA	F	Hispanic	Free lunch	No	choir	Yes
13	FRAIRE	ABRAHAM	M	Hispanic	Free lunch	No	choir	Yes
14	FROST	CHARLES	M	White not Hispanic	Not low income	No	none	No
15	GOMEZ	ADRIAN	M	Hispanic	Free lunch	Yes	none	No
16	GREENE	BRAD	M	White not Hispanic	Not low income	No	none	No
17	HAMILTON	AMBER M	F	White not Hispanic	Free lunch	No	none	No
18	HERNANDES	MIGUEL	M	Hispanic	Not low income	No	band	Yes
19	IRIGOYEN	ANTONIO	M	Hispanic	Not low income	No	none	No
20	IRIGOYEN	DANIEL	M	Hispanic	Free lunch	Yes	band	Yes

Figure 5.2. Student database with additional columns added

So we want to know if our school music programs are attracting similar proportions of students who are English Learners and students who are not. We will take advantage of an Excel function called "pivot table." When we illustrated the student database above, we showed only twenty student records. In our next demonstrations, we will analyze data on 869 students.

In the tab at the top of the screen, click the Insert tab. Highlight the range of columns that contain the data in which you are interested, in this case, ENGLISH LEARNER and MUSIC PARTICIPATION. In the process, of course, you will highlight any columns in between those two (ones you do not need in the analysis), but do not worry about that for the moment. Later we will have the chance to select just the columns in which we are interested. The top portion of your spreadsheet should look like figure 5.3.

Then, click Pivot Table. On our Excel spreadsheet, it appears in the upper left-hand corner of the screen, once you have clicked the Insert tab. A small Create Pivot Table window (figure 5.4) will appear, showing (in Excel language) the area you have selected. As we write this, for example, the window shows the name of our file, followed by an exclamation point, then this: $F$1:$I$8. All that means is that our pivot table can analyze any data from column F, row 1 to column I, row 8.

Click OK. A new sheet appears. On the right is the Pivot Table Field List (figure 5.5).

Here is where we must proceed carefully. The outcome with which we are concerned (some people call this the dependent variable) is music participation. Merely for the sake of consistency, we want our pivot table to look like our chart above (table 5.1). We will have one column for each classification, English Learner: Yes, and English Learner: No. So we click on English Learner and drag it to the box called Column Labels at the bottom of the Pivot Table Field List. Immediately, you should see, in the upper left portion of the screen, a cell that says, Column Labels and then rows that say English Learner, Yes, and No. Then, we click on Music Participation, and drag it to the box called Row Labels at the bottom of the Pivot Table Field List (figure 5.6).

FIRSTNAME	SEX	ETHNICITY	LUNCH	ENGLISH LEARNER	MUSIC PROGRAM	MUSIC PARTICIPATION
ABEL	M	Hispanic	Free lunch	No	band	Yes
JAVIER M	M	Hispanic	Free lunch	No	none	No
MATTHEW	M	Hispanic	Free lunch	No	choir	Yes

Figure 5.3. Highlighting columns that contain the data of interest

Using a Spreadsheet Pivot Table to Do an Equity Audit for Social Justice   79

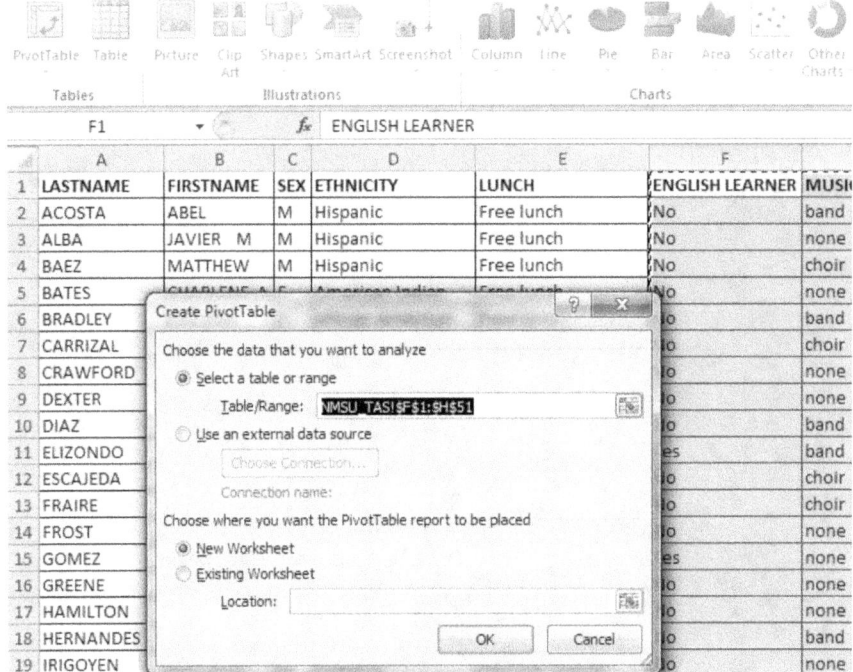

Figure 5.4.   The Create Pivot Table window

Immediately, you should see, on the upper left portion of the screen, a cell with the title Count of Music Participation, and below that a row title No, and a row title Yes. Below, we will tell you what to do if it does not say, "Count of."

Now, we need Excel to do our analysis of data on 869 students' records. To get numbers in our pivot table, we click again on Music Participation (our dependent variable) and drag it to the box called Values at the bottom of our Pivot Table Field List. If it does not say Count of, follow these steps: first, click on the menu item Analyze. Under Analyze you will see the selection Active Field. In Active Field, you will see the words Field Settings. Click on it (figure 5.7).

The Value Field Settings window will open (figure 5.8). From the Value Field Settings window, select Count. Once you select Count, you should get a table with the numbers shown in figure 5.9 below.

To make our lives easier, we should now label the pivot table rows and columns to remind us of what they mean. Remember that our columns refer to whether students are English Learners. So we can go into the cell of the spreadsheet that says, Column Labels and replace it with "English Learners?"

Figure 5.5. The Pivot Table Field List showing the columns we highlighted

Figure 5.6. Selecting our Column and Row Labels and our values

The row below English Learners now has Yes and No columns to indicate whether a student is an English Learner or not. Then, we click in the Row Labels cell and replace it with "Music Participation?" (figure 5.9).

Excel has now nicely counted our student records and tallied them based on the four possibilities: (1) English Learner in a music program, (2) English Learner not in a music program, (3) not-an-English-Learner but in a music program, (4) and not-an-English-Learner not in a music program.

At the risk of sounding like our colleague at the cocktail party above, let us look at what a couple of the numbers mean. Under the column: English

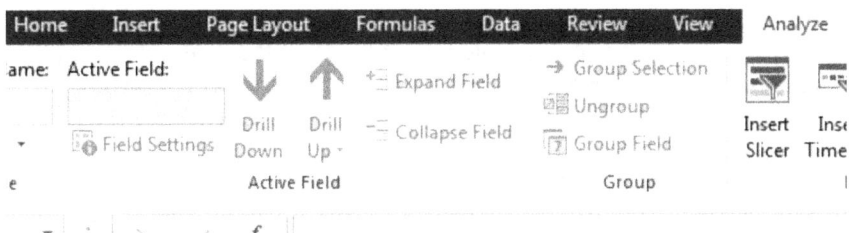

Figure 5.7. Selecting Active Field from Analyze menu

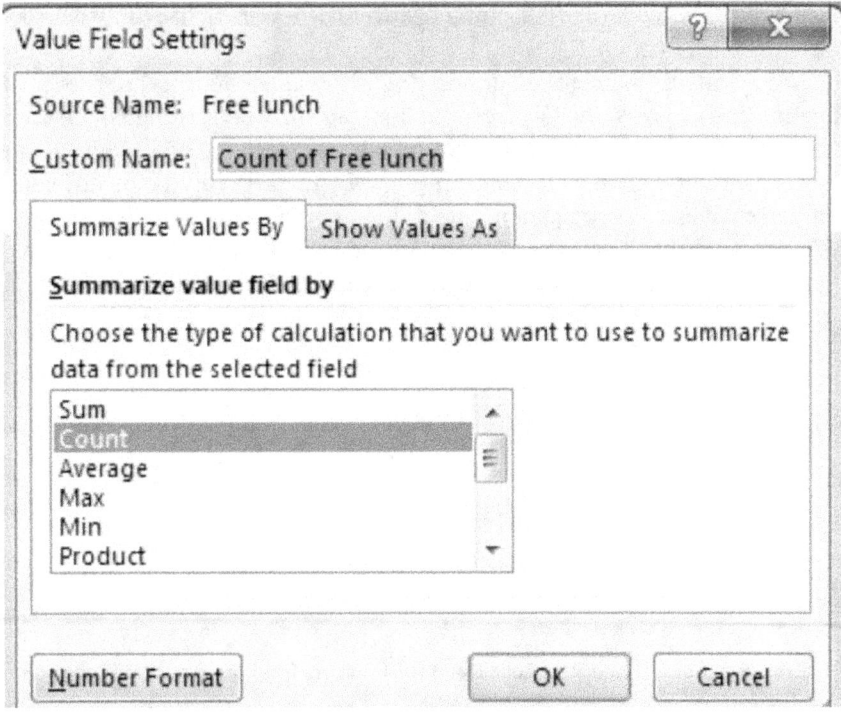

Figure 5.8. Selecting Count in the Value Field Settings window

Learners, No, we see the number 375. That means that of the 869 students in our database, 375 are not English Learners and not participating in a music program. One column over from the 375, under the Yes, we see a 59. That means that 59 of our 869 students are English Learners and not participating in a music program. One column over, under Grand Total, we see a 434, the total of the 375 and the 59. Of our 869 students, 434 are not participating in a music program.

Now, you need only ask Excel to calculate the percentages for you. Just as we did in tables 5.1 and 5.2, we divide the subset of each population (those participating in a music program) by the total number of students in that population. We ask Excel to divide the number of Non-English-Learner students in a music program (column b, row 4) by the total number of Non-English-Learner students (column b, row 5). Let us show that percentage in column b, row 8: (1) We place our cursor in cell b8 and (2) enter the division formula: =b6/b7.

We copy from cell b8 to cell c8 to repeat the calculations, this time for English Learner students. That gives us two decimal values. To convert them to percentages, we merely click the percent button in the Percentage box. Use the left and right arrows at the right of the Percentage box to carry our percentages out to more (left-pointing arrow) or fewer (right-pointing arrow) decimal places (figure 5.10).

We see that 51 percent of our non-English-Learner students are participating in a music program; 43 percent of our students who are English Learners are. This is a difference in participation rates between the two groups. Is the difference large enough to concern you? To us, a twenty-point difference in percentages of participation would definitely be serious; a ten-point difference might well raise some concerns. You and your school community must judge whether this 8 percent difference should concern you and what, if anything, you should do about it.

	A	B	C	D
1	Count of MUSIC PARTICIPATION	English Learners		
2	Music Participation?	No	Yes	Grand Total
3	No	375	59	434
4	Yes	390	45	435
5	Grand Total	765	104	869

Figure 5.9.   Column and Row Labels and the numbers from our pivot table analysis

A CAUTION ABOUT SMALL POPULATIONS

As wonderful as we believe percentages are, there is one place where you must proceed judiciously: when your population is very small. Analyzing percentages on small populations can lead to unwise conclusions—and you can err in either of two directions.

First, do not leap to big conclusions with small populations. With very small populations, one small difference can lead to a huge percentage change. Suppose, for example, a school staff is analyzing dropout rates and has only five members of a particular population. Three of them drop out of school, yielding a 60 percent dropout rate for that population. It looks terrible. Yet if only two had dropped out (a change of one student), the dropout rate would be 40 percent, a substantial difference from 60 percent. When working with small populations, you should think carefully before reacting to small percentages and percentage changes.

Second, do not totally ignore percentages on small populations either. We mentioned above that social justice does not happen without resistance. You can expect people who want to resist change for social justice to argue for discounting data on small populations. But students from small populations can be marginalized, and if we care about social justice, we should care about those students as much as the others. While we should be cautious about percentages on small populations, that doesn't mean we should ignore them totally.

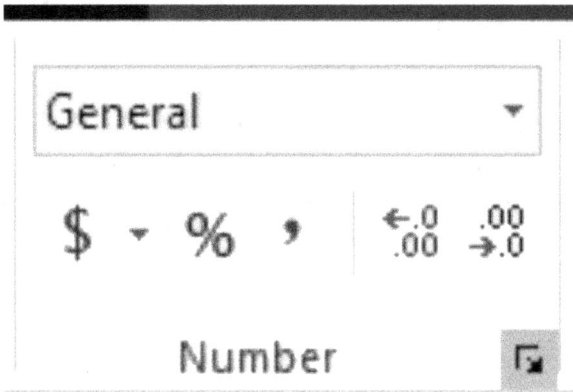

Figure 5.10. Changing decimal values to percentages and selecting the number of decimal places

A good tactic here is to examine several years of data to see if you can see any patterns, positive or negative. And, as we said above, it is always incumbent on leaders to be deliberate, intentional, accountable, and reflective, as well as willing to take risks, learn new skills, and create a culture of change. At this point, we return to the seven steps suggested by Skrla et al. (2004) and Skrla, McKenzie, and Scheurich (2009).

SEVEN STEPS TOWARD EQUITY

Let us look in more depth at each of the seven steps listed above.

1. Create a committee of relevant stakeholders. Relevant stakeholders may include teachers, parents, community members, business leaders, or students (provided students are mature enough to understand and contribute meaningfully to the process). Members of the committee should be well respected. Teachers who are influential, such as those who are representatives of teacher unions or other important groups, would be good additions. District and campus leaders and parent and advocacy group representatives from the community should also be included.

Advocacy group representatives could come from the Parent Teacher Association/Organization (PTA/PTO), League of Latin American Citizens (LULAC), National Hispanic Education Coalition (MALDEF), National Association for the Advancement of Colored People (NAACP), National Urban League (NUL), National Indian Education Association (NIEA), National Congress of American Indians (NCAI), Asian American Legal Defense and Education Fund (AALDEF), Asian American Justice Center (AAJC), or others that represent marginalized people.

2. Next, present the findings from your analysis(es) to the committee. We suggest providing graph paper or chart sheets, so that committee members themselves are able to graph percentages or frequencies on paper, using color codes or other methods to identify gaps that may concern them.

3. The committee should now have an open discussion about any equity gaps as they surface. This is the time when educational leaders from other districts who have gone through successful equity audits and have seen improvement in target areas similar to yours can help with analysis and advice. Other experts could also be brought to the school.

An important part of this step is to have an excellent facilitator, since difficult and sensitive issues can arise. The facilitator should be able to communicate effectively about issues of equity, like race, ethnicity, religion, ability, socioeconomic status, sexual orientation and identity, and any other issues that need attention.

Those in attendance must feel that they can speak and be heard with respect and dignity, and the facilitator must be perceptive about not allowing the discussion to become trapped in negative, nonproductive ways. A skilled facilitator will know how to provide support for discussion of difficult issues while moving the committee forward in a positive way.

We add here an additional suggestion to those of Skrla et al. (2004) and Skrla, McKenzie, and Scheurich (2009): consider carefully before you decide on the *cause(s)* of the gap(s). If the numbers suggest to you that you might have a problem with equity, your problem-solving work is just beginning. The *numbers* are not what you need to fix; the *cause* of the numbers is. Your job now is to ferret out the cause(s).

We fear that the last couple of decades of accountability pressures have impelled educators to focus on the numbers. Numbers, after all, are what end up in the newspapers. But Love (2009) cautioned about improvement-minded educators who were good at using data to locate problems "but would often respond to those problems prematurely, before they explored fully what practices in their system might be contributing to the problem and what research has to say about the problem" (p. 65).

You must diagnose further to determine the best course of action. Just as a high temperature or a stomach pain suggests that there might be a health problem, the solution is not merely to lower the high temperature (eat some ice chips) or reduce the pain (start a morphine drip). We must investigate to locate the source(s) of the indicators and promising treatment(s). In addition, Love's excellent little book (2009) details steps to intelligent problem solving, once your data reveal that you may have a problem.

Chapters in a companion book to this one (Ivory & Christman, 2019) can help with the exploration. Three chapters that come to mind all focus on the iPad. Wilbur and colleagues describe technology that can assist with classroom observations. Lochmiller and Lester explain how free software can facilitate qualitative inquiry (a good approach to exploring sources of problems). Badgett tells how software can help you search for research literature relevant to your problem.

4. After open discussion and with a skilled facilitator still present, the committee should move toward potential solutions. Committee members should discuss the likelihood of each solution's success and the strengths, weaknesses, and costs of each solution. Then, the committee should commit to one or more solutions.

5. The next step is for actual implementation of the solutions. This process is one that must happen with sensitivity to the local context and with commitment from stakeholders.

6. The educational leader for the committee must then monitor implementation of the solutions and collect evidence of the results (returning to the pivot tables or whatever other analytical tools you began with) and share them with the committee for evaluation.

7. Celebrate successes and/or return to step three of the process. If the solution or solutions have been successful, then there are certainly reasons to celebrate. If the solutions are not successful, then the committee needs to return to step three or four and move forward from there.

Many schools and districts perform these steps or parts of these steps annually as part of their planning. Schools and districts can make equity audits a routine part of the planning process.

EQUITY TRAPS

When we plan for, conduct, and evaluate equity audits, we can become entangled in equity traps. Here we mention some traps and some skills for avoiding them. To describe these traps and skills, we rely heavily on the work of Skrla, McKenzie, and Scheurich (2009) from their book, *Using Equity Audits to Create Equitable and Excellent Schools*.

Equity Trap #1: Seeing Only Deficits

Deficit thinking is one way to derail an equity audit. Unfortunately, there are a number of administrators and teachers, even parents, who get trapped in deficit thinking. Valencia (1997) described deficit thinking in these words: "A theory that posits that the student who fails in school does so principally because of internal deficits or deficiencies. Such deficiencies manifest, it is alleged, in limited intellectual abilities, linguistic shortcomings, lack of motivation to learn, and immoral behavior" (p. 2).

There are many administrators and teachers who avoid deficit thinking. Unfortunately, some get caught in it. They may see students and parents as genetically or culturally inferior, as not caring about education, or as belonging to groups that are unmotivated or prone to bad behavior.

Skill Needed to Avoid Equity Trap #1

Educational leaders must reframe the perspectives of those who hold deficit views of students and their families. They must expose such deficit holders to the realities of the funds of knowledge (Moll et al., 1992) their students and families hold. McKenzie and Scheurich (2004) discuss three ways to reframe our understandings of our students and their families: neighborhood walks, oral histories, and three-way conferencing. They also provide specifics for how to carry them out. Put succinctly, there must be repeated and honest efforts to establish alliances with families and community members in the education of their children (Skrla, McKenzie, & Scheurich, 2009).

Equity Trap #2: Erasing Race and Culture

Racial erasure (hooks, 1992) is "the sentimental idea . . . that racism would cease to exist if everyone would forget about race and just see each other as human beings who are the same" (p. 12). Racial and cultural erasure implies that these characteristics are not worthy of thought and that we have to ignore them or put them aside to be able to see someone as a human being.

Skill Needed to Avoid Equity Trap #2

We need to become more racially and culturally cognizant. We need to learn more about ourselves and our own beliefs, both conscious and unconscious, and how they are related to our culture and upbringing. Brown (2006) has particularly good advice on how to reflect on our own beliefs. One way to become more aware and respectful of race and culture is by using learning groups to help us. These groups allow us to explore various books, films, articles, stories, editorials, and virtual spaces to discuss and study how we view race, ethnicity, and culture (Skrla, McKenzie, & Scheurich, 2009).

Equity Trap #3: Rationalizing Bad Behavior and Unfair Practices

Some teachers do not treat students fairly and with care. Instead, they continue to use practices in their classrooms that are not successful and result in preventing students from learning. The problem, these teachers posit, is the students, not the teacher. They see the problem outside themselves. Such a mindset causes teachers to forego self-reflection, and they thus do not change or even question their practices and beliefs (Skrla, McKenzie, & Scheurich, 2009).

Skill Needed to Avoid Equity Trap #3

When teachers become self-reflective, they are more likely to change their practices and beliefs. However, one cannot simply tell someone to become self-reflective. One way to encourage self-reflection is through the use of journals; daily journaling allows us to see how and what we think. Another way to encourage self-reflection is through a critical friend (Costa, 1993). Such a friend can ask the questions that need to be asked, questions that require self-reflection. Further, we can videotape our teaching and speaking. We can learn from our videotape how we present ourselves, our beliefs, and our behaviors to others, especially students.

Equity Trap #4: Norming the Negative

This trap refers to using group pressure on school members to normalize negative practices, behaviors, and beliefs. Such negativity can permeate the whole school, making negativity the norm for school climate. Such negativity is often done unconsciously and usually starts with a group of teachers or staff members talking negatively about a student or his or her family. If a counter opinion is offered by someone not part of the group, that person's thinking is criticized as "not really knowing about the problem," that is, the student or the student's family. The person is *normed* into the group's opinions. Such norming also occurs with new teaching practices and efforts to involve the community in the school. Such negative norming keeps the school climate in a status quo and change efforts are nearly impossible (Skrla, McKenzie, & Scheurich, 2009).

Skill Needed to Avoid Equity Trap #4

Educational leaders need to be skillful in creating a school that is thoroughly collaborative in nature, one in which practices, beliefs, and behaviors are in the open, are transparent. Such transparency will make deficit beliefs, unsuccessful practices, and inappropriate behaviors visible. Only then can transformation take place.

Teaching and learning tours as described by Skrla, McKenzie, and Scheurich (2009, chap. 10) are good ways not only to promote professional development, but to also provide chances for teachers to gather in small groups and debrief. In this manner, teachers have opportunities to become aware of their own beliefs and see how these beliefs inform their behaviors and practices. The situation becomes ripe for change.

ASPIRE, ASSESS, AND MOVE FORWARD

Educators are idealists, generally. We imagine that by our efforts we can make life better for people everywhere, in all kinds of ways. We aspire to make the world a more just place. This is a good thing. Our reach must exceed our grasp so that we remain energized and committed day after day. At the same time, our glorious hopes are not enough to ensure success. We must pursue justice with high hopes. But we must also take hard looks at our current situations, ascertain where we are with regard to our ideals, and draw on evidence to monitor our efforts to improve. Combining the analytical power of Excel pivot tables with the practical suggestions we have provided for moving forward can help us make our schools more just for everyone.

REFERENCES

Blackmore, J. (2009). Leadership for social justice: A transnational dialogue. *Journal of Research on Leadership Education, 4*(1), 1–10. Retrieved from http:www.ucea.org/jrle.

Brooks, J. S., & Miles, M. (2006). From scientific management to social justice . . . and back again? Pedagogical shifts in the study and practice of educational leadership. *International Electronic Journal for Leadership in Learning, 10*, article 21. Retrieved from http://www.ucalgary.ca/iejll.

Brown, K. M. (2006). Leadership for social justice and equity: Evaluating a transformative framework and andragogy. *Educational Administration Quarterly, 42*, 700–745.

Costa, A. (1993). Through the lens of a critical friend. *Educational Leadership, 51*(2), 49–51.

Furman, G. (2012). Social justice leadership as praxis: Developing capacities through preparation programs. *Educational Administration Quarterly, 48*(2), 191–229.

Gewirtz, S. (1998). Conceptualizing social justice in education: Mapping the territory. *Journal of Education Policy, 13*, 469–484.

Goldfarb, K. P., & Grinberg, J. (2002). Leadership for social justice: Authentic participation in the case of a community center in Caracas, Venezuela. *Journal of School Leadership,12*, 157–173.

Gorski, P. (2013). *Reaching and teaching students in poverty: Strategies for erasing the opportunity gap.* New York: Teachers College Press.

Green. T. L. (2017). Community-based equity audits: A practical approach for educational leaders to support equitable community-school improvements. *Educational Administration Quarterly, 53*(1), 3–39.

hooks, b. (1992). *Black looks: Race and representation.* Cambridge, MA: South End.

Ivory, G., & Christman, D. (Eds.). (2019). *Leading with technologies: Improving performance for educators.* Lanham, MD: Rowman & Littlefield.

Love, N. (2009). *Using data to improve learning for all: A collaborative inquiry approach.* Thousand Oaks, CA: Corwin.

McKenzie, K. B., Christman, D. E., Hernandez, F., Fierro, E., Capper, C. A., Dantley, M., González, M. L., & Scheurich, J. J. (2008). From the field: A proposal for educating leaders for social justice. *Educational Administration Quarterly, 44*, 111–138.

McKenzie, K. B., & Scheurich, J. J. (2004). Equity traps: A useful construct for preparing principals to lead schools that are successful with racially diverse students. *Educational Administration Quarterly, 40*(5), 601–632.

Moll, L. C., Amanti, C., Neff, D., & Gonzalez, N. (1992). Funds of knowledge for teaching: Using a qualitative approach to connect homes and classrooms. *Theory into Practice, 31*(2), 132–141.

Scanlan, M. (2013). A learning architecture: How school leaders can design for learning social justice. *Educational Administration Quarterly, 49*(2), 348–391.

Scheurich, J., & Skrla, L. (2003). *Leadership for equity and excellence: Creating high achievement classrooms, schools, and districts*. Thousand Oaks, CA: Corwin.

Skrla, L., McKenzie, K. B., & Scheurich, J. J. (2009). *Using equity audits to create equitable and excellent schools*. Thousand Oaks, CA: Corwin Press.

Skrla, L., Scheurich, J. J., Garcia, J., & Nolly, G. (2004). Equity audits: A practical leadership tool for developing equitable and excellent schools. *Educational Administration Quarterly, 40*, 135–163.

Skrla, L., Scheurich, J. J., Garcia, J., & Nolly, G. (2010). Equity audits: A practical leadership tool for developing equitable and excellent schools. In C. Marshall & M. Oliva (Eds.), *Leadership for social justice* (2nd ed., pp. 259–283). Boston: Allyn & Bacon.

Theoharis, G. (2007). Social justice educational leaders and resistance: Toward a theory of social justice leadership. *Educational Administration Quarterly, 43*(2), 221–258.

University Council for Educational Administration. (2014). Powerful learning experience 6: Conducting an equity audit. In *Preparing Leaders to Support Diverse Learners: LSDL Module Development Program*. Retrieved from http://ucealee.squarespace.com/conducting-an-equity-audit/.

Valencia, R. R. (1997). *The evolution of deficit thinking: Educational thought and practice*. London: Falmer.

Chapter Six

Technology, Ethics, and School Leadership

Scott McLeod

KEY POINTS IN THIS CHAPTER

- Numerous ethical issues accompany the deployment and integration of learning technologies in P–12 school systems.
- The ethical paradigms of *justice*, *critique*, *care*, and *the profession* can help school leaders analyze various school technology leadership scenarios.
- The four ethical paradigms often work in concert but also sometimes may contradict each other, resulting in school leaders having to make some very difficult decisions.
- Solutions are dependent on the ethical lenses, perspectives, and dispositions of school leaders and their communities—and on which factors carry the most weight with them.
- School leaders should regularly discuss various technology scenarios and ethical paradigms with relevant stakeholders in their communities.

Many schools across the world are working steadily to integrate learning technologies into their learning and teaching practices. Students and educators using new computing devices, digital platforms, and online environments in their day-to-day learning work gives rise to a whole host of new leadership and organizational considerations, including areas that may be of ethical concern. This chapter highlights some of those areas and offers a few lenses for thinking about them that may be useful to school leaders and the educational leadership faculty members who prepare them.

School administrators and other educators are no strangers to ethical issues that may arise in their schools, of course. Nearly every day a multitude of incidents require central office administrators, principals, teachers, counselors, librarians, and other school staff to think and act in ways that are both professional and ethical. As they address these incidents, it's helpful to have some frameworks to guide their thinking and decision making.

FOUR ETHICAL PARADIGMS

In their landmark text, *Ethical Leadership and Decision Making in Education*, Shapiro and Stefkovich (2016) outlined four key ethical paradigms that school administrators can use to analyze and reflect upon the daily occurrences that require them to exercise ethical and moral leadership. The four ethical frames of justice, critique, care, and professional standards each provide valuable lenses and perspectives for school leaders' decision making. Each of these paradigms is briefly described in the paragraphs that follow.

The ethical paradigm that often comes to mind when we think about school systems is *the ethic of justice*. This ethic focuses on laws, rules, policies, and rights and is primarily concerned with issues of fairness, equity, liberty, freedom, and balancing the rights of individuals with the rights of the many (Strike, 2006). The ethic of justice views "social relationships as a type of a social contract where the individual . . . gives up some rights for the good of the whole or for social justice" (Shapiro & Stefkovich, 2016, p. 11). Society teaches individuals how to behave through communal understandings of what is proper and appropriate (p. 11).

School administrators who use an ethic of justice focus on fairly applying the rules and policies that currently exist. They try to treat everyone the same and do their best to ensure that the procedures used to address daily school scenarios are uniformly applied. An emphasis is placed on following the rules in order to optimize the chance of fair outcomes for the most people.

In contrast, *the ethic of critique* asks school administrators to critically reflect on laws, rules, and policies and inquire whether the processes that created them are just, right, and fair. Shapiro and Stefkovich (2016) noted that the ethic of critique is deeply rooted in critical theory and it focuses on inequities related to social class, race, gender, sexual identity, and other potential categories of concern. The ethic of critique asks educators to recognize that schools often reproduce societal inequities and poses difficult questions regarding how rules and policies are made—who benefits, who has power, and whose voices are silenced (p. 15).

School administrators who use an ethic of critique focus on the fairness of the rules themselves. Instead of simply applying the policies or procedures that exist, they critically reflect on what drove the creation of the policies in the first place, who the policies are intended to cover, who may be explicitly or implicitly advantaged or disadvantaged by the policies, whether there is uneven application of procedures, whether unfair results seem to accrue due to the policies, and so on.

Many educators are familiar with the third ethic, *the ethic of care*. Rooted in a concern for others and the needs of young people, this ethic asks school leaders to focus on relationships, human connection (Beck, 1994), and "multiple voices in the decision-making process" (Shapiro & Stefkovich, 2016, p. 17) rather than simply following designated rules, operating procedures, and hierarchical command structures. Noddings (1992) articulated that "the first job of the schools is to care for our children" (p. xiv). However, it is not enough for leaders to care; others' perceptions of that caring are critically important for building relationships and trust.

In school systems that can be large, bureaucratic, and often dehumanizing, the ethic of care asks administrators to focus on the people whom they serve. Instead of uniformly following policies, school leaders who use an ethic of care note when those rules or procedures don't seem to make much sense, perhaps make exceptions, mitigate negative consequences due to individual circumstances, and so on. These school leaders also emphasize relationships, determine if others perceive a lack of care or trust, and may recognize that keeping others engaged sometimes can be more important than the application of a particular rule or policy.

The fourth ethical paradigm described by Shapiro and Stefkovich (2016) is *the ethic of the profession*. Numerous sets of school leadership standards list ethics and professional norms as primary concerns for educational administrators (see, e.g., AASA, 2018; NASSP, 2013). They typically articulate that school leaders should act ethically and professionally in all aspects of their professional lives and be good role models for other educators and children. These state and national professional standards often incorporate—explicitly or implicitly—the first three ethical paradigms described above (Shapiro & Stefkovich, 2016).

School administrators who use an ethic of the profession ask themselves what the relevant standards, norms, and best practices for school leaders say about situations that arise in their school settings. They also identify their own personal and professional ethical codes and work to reconcile those with leadership standards and norms and the situations that face them on a daily basis (Shapiro & Stefkovich, 2016, p. xv). This work usually requires the blending of elements from the other three ethical lenses.

With some basic ethical frameworks in hand, school leaders can use them to think about a variety of technology-related scenarios that commonly arise in schools. Note that the four ethical paradigms described above often work in concert but also sometimes may contradict each other. This can result in school leaders having to make some very difficult decisions as they decide which aspects of a given school issue deserve greater weight and consideration. Inevitably, other school stakeholders may disagree or be disappointed, perhaps because they believe that other ethical paradigms should be given higher priority.

SCENARIO 1: STUDENT TECHNOLOGY ACCESS

Carol Smithson is the new superintendent of the Bedford School District. Her district's technology team includes a chief technology officer (CTO), four support technicians, and three technology integration coaches. Bedford High School serves 1,950 students from primarily low-income neighborhoods in the downtown area. The other high school in the district has 1,400 students and generally serves more affluent neighborhoods in a rapidly growing suburb. Carol's incoming charge from the school board is to increase student test scores and successfully manage the influx of new suburban students and parents.

At a meeting with Carol and her CTO, the principal of Bedford High expresses his appreciation for the district's support of the school's new 1:1 laptop initiative. The principal also brings to their attention a recent article on "the homework gap," which notes that five million American households lack reliable, high-speed internet access, compromising their children's ability to complete digital and online homework assignments. A recent Bedford High survey shows that about one-third of its students struggle with home internet access. He asks the district to consider becoming an internet service provider (ISP) for its students and families.

Although Carol isn't opposed to the idea, she also knows that other learning and teaching programs are underway. She's particularly worried about taking energy and attention away from the district's new Multi-Tiered Systems of Support (MTSS) program. She's also not sure that she wants to take on the challenges that will arise from parents at the other high school who don't see the need for this initiative and from local, private ISPs who will be concerned about erosion of their market share and revenue generation. She wonders if teachers can simply assign less digital homework or if students can just visit their local libraries.

This scenario highlights the issue of *student technology access*, which still remains an issue in many households, particularly for families in traditionally underserved communities. Many school systems view their internal 1:1 technology initiatives as digital-equity programs that aim to combat this "digital divide." Some school districts are going further and are working with their local communities to find ways to increase high-speed internet access at home for their students. Given the pervasiveness of the internet in our lives these days, it does little good to send children home with computers if they can't get connected online.

If Carol approaches this situation from an ethic of justice, she may focus on the issues of achievement and equity. If so, she may determine that the district's MTSS initiative is more important than the district's technology initiative for boosting student test scores and keeping schools off the state watch list. That calculus is commonly made in numerous school systems, even those that believe that technology fluencies and new information literacies are important. Test score considerations are simply more dominant in our current accountability era. Accordingly, the burden is on students and families to make necessary accommodations.

However, Carol also could approach this issue from an ethic of care. Putting herself in the shoes of her students and families, she could empathize with their lack of internet access, gather more information about where "homework gaps" exist, talk to students and parents about the impacts of their lack of technology access, and map out neighborhoods' proximity to libraries and other sites with free internet access points for youth and families. She also could solicit teachers' creative ideas for addressing students' lack of access without discouraging digital homework and assignments.

If Carol approaches this issue from an ethic of critique, she may find herself questioning why the access divide exists in the first place. She could advocate for greater state and federal funding and programming to help boost technology access for low-income families. She could work with local businesses and government offices to increase the number of free internet access points and workspaces for local youth. And—like the schools in Albemarle County, Virginia; Coachella Valley, California; and Boulder County, Colorado—she could decide to tackle the multiyear dialogue around becoming an ISP, at least for her low-income neighborhoods.

If Carol looks to the ethics of her profession, the American Association of School Administrators (AASA) code of ethics for superintendents states that they should "[make] the education and well-being of students the fundamental value of all decision making" and "[pursue] appropriate measures to correct those laws, policies, and regulations that are not consistent with sound educational goals or that are not in the best interest of children" (AASA, 2018). The International Society for Technology in Education (ISTE) Standards for Education Leaders state that administrators should "ensure all students have access to the technology and connectivity necessary to participate in authentic and engaging learning opportunities" (ISTE, 2018).

SCENARIO 2: STUDENT TECHNOLOGY USE

Richard and Ronaldo have been best friends since second grade when they were in Mrs. Moran's class together at Forest View Elementary. Now eighth graders at Lake Shore Middle School, they've gradually drifted apart academically. Richard is in the Gifted and Talented program and is taking algebra and other advanced courses. Ronaldo has been struggling with his classes and his teachers are worried about both his grades and test scores in several subjects. Although they don't have their core classes together, Richard and Ronaldo share several electives and a lunch period and are on the same local baseball team.

Lake Shore is in its third year of a 1:1 computing initiative and gives every student a MacBook Air laptop. The school has been on an A-B block schedule for many years, with four blocks of class time each day to allow for longer periods of learning. The A and B schedules alternate every other day and each student takes eight courses per year. In order to boost reading and math scores on the state assessment, Principal Wendy Park recently implemented a mandatory class rotation for every student in the school called What I Need (WIN).

For academically struggling students, the WIN class is used for remediation and intervention. Teachers determine what students like Ronaldo need to work on, who then engage in additional direct instruction and tutoring with a teacher or use their laptops to complete self-paced, vendor-purchased, adaptive learning software modules in reading and math. Students like Richard who are doing better academically have opportunities in WIN to engage in collaborative enrichment and extension projects such as building robots and rockets, learning how to code, and creating multimedia stories that are shared with the community.

One day during lunch, Richard comments about how excited he is for the day's WIN period. The class designed their own houses using specialized software and today they are going to get feedback from local architects and building contractors. Ronaldo is considerably less enthused. He knows that he will be doing yet another boring, self-paced, software-driven literacy activity for ninety minutes. He wishes that he had a chance to design houses and build robots and rockets with Richard and remembers fondly being on both the First Lego League robotics and Destination Imagination teams when he was at Forest View Elementary.

This scenario highlights the issue of *student technology use*, sometimes referred to as the "secondary digital divide." Even when students have access to learning technologies, there can be great disparities in how they are used. Some students like Richard get to do things with computers, while other students like Ronaldo have things done to them by computers. Student agency and deeper learning are important concerns when it comes to student technology use. Influential technology pioneer Seymour Papert noted long ago that students should be programming computers rather than being programmed by them (Blikstein, 2013).

If Wendy adopts an ethic of justice, she may determine that bringing up Ronaldo's achievement on traditional testing and grading metrics is most important. The school likely is judged by its state assessment scores, after all. However, if she adopts the ethics of care and critique, she may find herself asking some difficult questions about whether accomplishment on those traditional metrics is enough for life success in today's global innovation society. In other words, she may find herself investigating which kids in her school get to build "future ready" skills such as collaboration, critical thinking, and problem solving and which ones don't.

The ethics of her profession may not provide specific guidance to Wendy in this instance. Similar to AASA, the NASSP code of ethics for secondary principals simply says that school leaders should "[make] the well-being and success of students the fundamental value in all decision-making and actions" (NASSP, 2013). The Association for Middle Level Education (AMLE) is a partner in the national Whole Child Initiative, which advocates for ensuring that (among other things) middle school students are "engaged in learning, supported by caring adults, and challenged by a well-balanced curriculum" (AMLE, 2018).

SCENARIO 3: STUDENT DATA PRIVACY AND COMMERCIALISM

Amanda Vallejo and Daryl Williams are the superintendent and technology director, respectively, of the Eagle Canyon School District, a small rural system with just four schools. A group of parents approaches them with concerns about the no-cost Google Apps for Education (GAFE) office suite used by the district. Specifically, the parents are concerned that Google is tracking students' email and online activity and using their data to build advertising profiles. The parents also are concerned about the lack of student data privacy protections and advertisements in many of the software tools and apps that teachers use in their classrooms.

Like thousands of other districts across the country, Eagle Canyon moved to GAFE several years ago because it was becoming too costly to maintain its own email servers and office suite licenses for all of its desktop and laptop computers, even with significant educational discounts. The district pays for several additional educational software systems but also has allowed teachers discretion regarding which free or low-cost technology tools they use with their students. The group of parents has requested that the district ramp up its student privacy protections and stop using GAFE and all non-district-vetted software tools.

This scenario highlights the issue of *student data privacy* and the attendant commercialism concerns that often accompany the use of "free" software tools by school systems and their educators. School budgets typically are tight and school leaders often want to foster innovative technology uses by teachers. However, there is an old saying that "if you're not paying for the product, you are the product" (Lewis, 2010; Michelson, Serra, & Weyergraf, 1979, p. 104).

Educational researchers have long chronicled the dangers of commercialism in schools (see, e.g., Molnar, 2005; Molnar & Boninger, 2015). Parents thus are rightfully concerned about the commercial messages that their children are exposed to at school. Similarly, numerous states have enacted new student data privacy protections, with Colorado's Student Data Transparency and Security Act (Colorado Department of Education, 2016) perhaps being the most stringent. Balancing district needs and goals with those of students and families often is a difficult challenge.

Amanda and Daryl can take an ethic of justice approach to the parents' concerns. They can explain their budget limitations and decision-making processes, cite the district's compliance with state and federal laws, and point to the fact that other districts are using GAFE with great success and with appropriate privacy assurances from Google. They can also institute some new rules and procedures for teachers' software selection, requiring that classroom educators only use district-approved technology tools or get permission to use software, apps, and websites not on the district's "white list."

An ethic of care approach may require different actions from Amanda and Daryl, however, in order to hear a wider span of perspectives. Amanda and Daryl may need to listen more deeply to the concerns of this small parent group to see if accommodations can be made for these families, and they may need to survey and interview the larger community of parents to determine if these concerns are widely or narrowly held. They also may need to hear from teachers and students about why and how they make their technology choices and what the potential impacts on learning and teaching might be of new rules, procedures, or limitations.

SCENARIO 4: CYBERBULLYING

After a national wave of "creepy clown" threats, a student at Whitewater High School posts on Twitter that "the concert choir with all their makeup are the only clowns we got around here." Whitewater principal George Weatherspoon suspends the student for several days, citing the district's policy against bullying and cyberbullying. He also gives one-day suspensions to twelve other students who "liked" the tweet, stating that they added their names to a list of people who agreed with and supported the bullying. Several parents of the students have appealed to the superintendent, Leslie Turner, asking her to overturn the suspensions.

This was not the first social media incident that George had dealt with this year. Two weeks earlier, he had given a student a one-day suspension for tweeting a picture of a teacher's car parked near a No Parking sign with an accompanying statement of "I hope Mr. Peterson gets towed." The month before that, George suspended a student for three days for posting "I hate Mrs. Carroll" on her Facebook page and inviting other students to chime in. Leslie wonders if the district's bullying and cyberbullying policy may need some clarification.

This scenario highlights the issue of *cyberbullying*, a concern that has received attention in recent years with the growth of smartphones, mobile computers, and social media platforms. Although research seems to indicate that online bullying tends to be less prevalent than in-person bullying (see, e.g., Common Sense Media, 2018; Przybylski & Bowes, 2017), the potential speed of growth and scale of cyberbullying incidents—along with frequent anonymity of the bullies—make this issue particularly vexing for school leaders. Compounding the issue is the fact that, as noted in chapter 4, students possess the right to have opinions and engage in off-campus speech. But social media blurs the line between when a student is off-campus and when not.

Leslie's review from an ethic of justice perspective likely will focus on whether George's discipline of the students for their social media posts was fair, appropriate, and legal. It is arguable whether any of the posts are sufficiently negative and pervasive to constitute "bullying," and it is possible and perhaps even likely that a court would find that George's enforcement of what he perceives to be school policies and state laws is a bit overzealous, particularly for the students who were disciplined for merely "liking" a post. Leslie can review relevant laws and policies with George and make clear her expectations regarding enforcement.

An ethics of care approach would involve Leslie and George discussing with the students why they posted what they did, how the school is trying to build community, what student and teacher rights and responsibilities are within that community, and what impacts the students' posts had on others. This approach would be less administrative, punitive, and rules oriented and more conversational, restorative, and community oriented. Of course, a combination of the justice and care perspectives may lead to the best possible resolution that addresses the concerns of all parties.

SCENARIO 5: SEXTING

After some pressure from Jevonte, her boyfriend and fellow high school sophomore, Makayla sends a nude photograph to him via the Snapchat app on their phones. Several months later—after what everyone agrees was an acrimonious breakup—Jevonte shows a screenshot of Makayla's picture to a few friends.

Word spreads quickly about Makayla's photo and eventually reaches the principal, Horace Taggart. Horace now must determine whether to suspend Jevonte and Makayla. He also must decide whether to refer them to the county prosecutor for potential charges under the state's child pornography law. As Horace considers his options, he also is cognizant that both students involved are low-income, African American children and he doesn't want to fuel the ongoing "school-to-prison pipeline" concerns that already exist in the community.

This scenario highlights the issue of student *sexting*, an activity that often raises legal concerns when done by minors. Sexting is the digital transmission of sexual messages or images—including nude photographs—to others. Although this may be acceptable when both the sender and recipient are legally consenting adults, sexting by underage youth often implicates them in state child-pornography and sexual-victimization laws. If messages or images are passed along to others in a school community, sexual harassment rules and policies also may come into play.

It would be simple for Horace to simply adopt an ethic of justice perspective and emphasize the rules and laws that are in place. In that case, he might try to discipline one or both students for violating school policies regarding inappropriate technology use and sexual harassment. He also would refer Jevonte—and perhaps Makayla under some states' laws—for criminal prosecution. Rules are rules, laws are laws, and Jevonte (and maybe Makayla) broke both.

It appears, however, that Horace has some concerns related to the ethics of care and critique. He's not sure that punishment is what is best for these children and he has some grave concerns about criminalizing their behavior. Consensual sexting and sending nude selfies to a partner don't seem like the sexual predation that the state law is trying to prevent. Jevonte probably deserves some disciplinary action for sharing Makayla's picture, and Makayla definitely needs some conversations about smarter ways to use technology and better protect herself. But both of those are a far cry from felony charges and possible criminal records.

Horace's concerns about feeding his community's "school-to-prison pipeline" likely would fall under the ethic of critique. Under this perspective, Horace could spark conversations with others about which student technology behaviors are criminal and which are merely ill-considered or immature. He also could advocate for changes at the state policy level that decriminalize certain activities by youth and thus reduce the possibility of children accruing a criminal record for what simply may be thoughtless adolescent behavior. Moreover, Horace could combat peer-to-peer pressuring behaviors that lead to students reluctantly sharing nude pictures with partners.

From an ethic of the profession perspective, Horace has an explicit professional obligation to follow the rules and policies of his district and the laws and regulations of his state. Folding in a perspective of critique, however, he also may need to consider how he should act when he feels that a particular law or rule is unjust or unfair.

SCENARIO 6: CURRICULUM, TECHNOLOGY SECURITY, AND PARENT OPT-OUT

A small but vocal group of parents in the Timberland School District is extremely concerned about the negative effects of digital technologies on their elementary age children. Some of them have no televisions or computers in their homes or reserve them only for adult use. Most of the rest implement very strict screen-time limits at home, preferring that their children read, play outside, and engage in other nontechnological recreational activities.

Timberland begins purchasing and using Chromebooks for students in an attempt to ensure that its graduates are technology fluent and information literate in today's digital and online environments. The parent group pushes back, complaining that digital homework assignments infringe on their parenting choices and that the district is forcing Chromebooks on their families. They request that the district discontinue its Chromebook initiative, either for their schools or the entire district. They also go directly to the school board with screenshots of "inappropriate" content and images that have slipped through the district's internet filter.

Margaret Tynall, Timberland's chief information officer, supports the district's desire to prepare "future ready" students and graduates. She also knows that the district is well ahead of others in the area when it comes to technology safety and security but that every internet filter can simultaneously underblock and overblock content. That is, some undesirable content makes it through and some desirable content is blocked, no matter what settings are chosen. She isn't exactly sure what to do but, given the increased oversight of the district's technology programs by the superintendent and school board, is beginning to suspect that her job is on the line if she doesn't figure it out.

This scenario highlights multiple issues related to *students and curriculum*, with a secondary emphasis on issues related to parenting and technology security. At the forefront is the issue of whether student use of school-provided computing devices is more akin to sex education, for which many states allow parent opt-out, or to science education and textbooks, for which states typically do not allow parent opt-out. Subsidiary concerns also exist regarding homework, family parenting choices, and the sufficiency of the district's internet filtering and blocking system.

In some ways this situation is similar to scenario 3 above. Most of the approaches available to Amanda and Daryl in that situation also are available to Margaret and her district in this one. What this scenario brings to the fore, however, is what happens when parent concerns are about fundamental student outcomes and modalities of learning rather than a few software choices that arguably could be made differently. In other words, the question here is how Margaret and the district should respond—ethically, professionally, and with due care—to parent requests to opt out of what the district views as essential learning and teaching.

Scenario 2 with Richard and Ronaldo asked whether schools themselves take seriously the task of preparing students for future readiness and life success. Here in the Timberland School District, that question goes one step further. The ultimate question here has nothing to do with digital homework or internet filtering; those are simply operational adjustments that may need to be made. The larger question in Timberland is not just whether the school system views future readiness as an important student outcome but whether its school leaders think it is imperative enough to persist even in the face of vocal pushback (at least from a few parents).

All four of the ethical perspectives presented in this chapter—justice, critique, care, and the profession—ask school leaders to reflect deeply on issues related to educational adequacy and equity. If some parents want to opt out their children from what the district views as essential curriculum and learning opportunities for the life success of its graduates, the district might decide to try and accommodate them (although it is an open question whether they should, given that it likely would not do so for science, math, or reading). Giving those parents "veto rights" over the future readiness of other parents, children, and schools in the district is another matter.

The larger question is beyond the scope of Margaret's position. The superintendent and the school board together determine how hard the district will fight for the life success of its graduates and for equitable opportunities for all students within the system. It is possible that they could adopt all four ethical perspectives, engage in all of the activities noted in scenario 3, and determine that most parents are in favor of the district's current path, yet still lack the courage to stand up to this vocal minority group of parents. If so, their graduates may suffer the long-term consequences of the district's willingness to sacrifice the many for the few.

If the district does fortify its college- and career-readiness backbone and stands firmly behind its chosen path, there are a variety of ways that its leaders could possibly accommodate these vocal parents while also holding steady on their overall objectives and desired student outcomes. These accommodations likely would not include allowing a small group of parents to dictate the actions of other families and schools that do not share their concerns. They might, however, include some opt-out options that only affected those specific children as long as that didn't create undue burdens for educators, other families, or the school system itself.

SCENARIO 7: SCHOOL SAFETY

Douglas McCormick is the assistant superintendent of Finance, Operations, and Technology for the Lewiston Schools. In the aftermath of numerous school shootings across the nation, he has been bombarded by vendors pitching school security products and services, including metal detectors, bulletproof doors, panic buttons, and emergency lockdown notification apps (Watters, 2018). Fearful parents also have asked the district to consider hiring armed guards, implement new lockdown procedures and active shooter training drills, and perhaps even arm teachers.

Recently a group of parents sent a marketing brochure to the superintendent and chair of the school board that described new digital camera security systems that have facial recognition software that can identify "people, objects, and even behaviors that could present safety threats" (Herold, 2018). The parents also want the district to invest in social media surveillance software that will allow the district to monitor all students' social media accounts "in the hopes of preventing mass shootings and student suicide" (Mullins, 2018). Douglas has been asked to give the district his recommendation about these new security technologies.

This scenario highlights the issue of *school safety*, a heightened concern for school administrators due to the visibility of several mass shootings in schools in recent years. Although research seems to indicate that schools tend to be safer now than in previous decades (see, e.g., Nicodemo & Petronio, 2018), the visibility and shock of these incidents has given rise to numerous calls to make schools safer.

School security vendors predictably have stepped up their marketing strategies, pitching a variety of products intended to assuage administrator and community concerns. Many of these products are costly but of dubious value (Schuppe, 2018), particularly given the infrequency of school mass shootings. Cost and viability often take a backseat, however, to vocal parents' fears and community demands to "do something" to keep their kids safe. Privacy concerns and the right of citizens to be free from suspicionless surveillance often are diminished as well in the wake of safety concerns (see, e.g., Schneier, 2003, 2018).

Under the ethical perspectives of care or the profession, Douglas might recommend that the district do everything it can to protect its students. However, he would be wise to pull in a variety of parent and community members, since it may be that a small but vocal group is dominating the conversation (as in scenario 6). School expenditures always involve trade-offs and opportunity costs. For instance, if money is spent on school safety and security products, that means fewer dollars for other curricular, extracurricular, and facilities projects that parents want to see happen. Responsible spending also falls under the ethics of care and the profession.

Additionally, Douglas probably would raise important questions about the desired balance between school security and student feelings of privacy and belonging. Surveillance of off-campus student communications—even if ostensibly for the good of the students and the school community—likely will erode students' positive feelings of trust and connection with the school. If Douglas and the district care about students' perceptions, they probably should bring in a variety of student, parent, and community perspectives before he makes recommendations in this area.

If Douglas used an ethic of critique, he might ask questions about why schools have to bear the brunt of the financial costs related to larger societal issues around privacy, safety, and gun control. He might even advocate for laws and funding streams that would protect school budgets, although there still would be larger societal trade-offs and opportunity costs, such as fewer monies for other educational priorities. Finally, from an ethic of justice perspective, Douglas would need to ensure that whatever new procedures the district put into place fell squarely within state and federal guidelines and legally required student protections.

SCENARIO 8: STUDENT LEARNING AND CREDIT RECOVERY

Like many school systems, the Maryville School District is struggling to increase its high school graduation rate. And like many school systems, Maryville has turned to commercial providers to create "credit recovery" pathways that allow academically struggling students to make up credits. Students in Maryville's alternative high school spend multiple hours per day logging into self-paced online courses and completing assignments. The school's few teachers check in with students, answer questions that arise, and do some tutoring when necessary.

Maryville has seen its graduation rate increase from 72 percent to 81 percent over the past five years, primarily due to its use of credit recovery. However, Nathan Bentley, the curriculum director, is concerned about the academic rigor of many of the courses and some anecdotes that he is hearing about low-quality student work. Nathan doesn't want to foreclose technology-facilitated learning choices for students who struggle with traditional classroom instruction but is facing increasing scrutiny about the credit recovery program. He notes that a large proportion of the students in credit recovery are students of color and/or from low-income families.

This scenario highlights the issue of *student learning* and access to high-quality curricula. Credit recovery programs have grown rapidly in recent years and graduation rates are up in many districts (Wexler, 2018). Advocates cite the personalized and competency-based aspects of many of these programs (Powell, Roberts, & Patrick, 2015). Critics cite concerns about program quality, particularly for learning models that involve students clicking through self-paced modules from commercial vendors (Malkus & Cummings, 2018).

At first glance the Maryville credit recovery program seems to satisfy ethics of care, justice, and profession concerns related to student success. The program was put in place to remedy graduation gaps and seems primarily to serve many of the district's academically struggling and often underserved students and families. Although the graduation rate is up, it may be that curricular quality of the credit recovery program is inferior and ultimately a disservice to the very students it is supposed to help. If Nathan and the district are serious about equity concerns, they will investigate the adequacy of student learning in the program.

If Nathan uses an ethic of critique perspective, he may begin to ask questions about the societal and school factors that caused the need for a credit recovery program in the first place. If adequate community and educational supports were in place, more students would be successful in the regular academic program and fewer students would need costly alternative technologies and approaches. The monies saved on credit recovery software could be spent in other areas to facilitate student success and perhaps even provide new learning opportunities that allow students to gain new skills and move ahead rather than simply catch up (see scenario 2).

SCENARIO 9: EXPECTATIONS FOR EDUCATORS' PROFESSIONALISM

After last year's passage of a community technology funding referendum, all teachers at Woodland K–8 School now have a classroom set of iPads for use with their students. The older students in fifth through eighth grades can even take their iPads home over the evenings and weekends. The school has invested heavily in its new student computing initiative, including a full-time technology integration coach and numerous professional learning opportunities to help teachers and their aides learn how to integrate the iPads into their classroom instruction.

Principal Sondra Hutton has heard from many teachers and parents that they are excited about the new learning experiences that students are receiving. However, a couple of teachers remain holdouts, rarely or never using the iPads in their classrooms. At her fall evaluation conference, kindergarten teacher Dorothy Frederick stated that she doesn't believe iPads are appropriate for young children and that, even if they were, her students aren't developmentally ready for such advanced technology. Similarly, Ben Battello has said to others that he's already an excellent fourth grade teacher and thus doesn't need the iPads in his classroom.

Another handful of teachers at Woodland are less visibly reluctant but they also aren't using technology very often in creative or meaningful ways. Their attendance at school-sponsored professional learning sessions is sporadic and they're mostly using technology in ways that either make their classes a little more efficient or replicate what they did before they had computers in their classrooms. Sondra wants to respect the teaching choices and professionalism of her staff but also wants to honor the community's technology investments and ensure that all students have experiences that help them gain new skills and technology fluencies.

This scenario highlights the issue of *teacher professionalism* and school expectations regarding educator development and the implementation of new learning and teaching endeavors. Every school technology initiative requires educators to learn new tools, skills, and strategies. School leaders must determine how best to provide learning opportunities for their classroom educators and how to structure supports and expectations appropriately to optimize organizational implementation and student outcomes. Teachers that decide to "opt out" of new programs, actively or passively, are frequently a challenge for school administrators.

These situations require school leaders who adopt an ethic of care to balance the needs of both students and teachers. Many educators are anxious or fearful about adopting new pedagogies and technologies, or are rightfully concerned about demands on their time and their lack of teaching efficacy while they are learners in a new area. Educators deserve all of the empathy and support structures that school leaders can provide. Simultaneously, however, administrators must keep the needs of students and the organization at the forefront.

From an ethic of justice perspective, this means that school leaders can't allow teachers to opt out of acquiring and implementing new techniques and strategies that the district believes will move learning forward. Hiring criteria, observation and evaluation rubrics, school vision and mission statements, and other organizational expectation structures should send strong messages about the types of learning experiences that are expected, and they should be accompanied by accountability mechanisms that ensure that desired experiences occur for students. As we have seen above, ethics of the profession require that we put the needs of students first.

CONCLUSION

Many schools and districts are giving their students access to personal computing devices, digital learning tools, and online environments in order to enhance their schoolwork and extend their learning beyond the school day. As they do so, a number of ethical concerns can arise that require them to consider their deeply held values as educators and communities. This chapter identified a few of those scenarios and attempted to provide some frameworks and suggestions for thinking about them.

There are no easy answers here. Solutions and pathways are dependent on the ethical lenses, perspectives, and dispositions of school leaders and their communities—and which factors carry the most weight with them. As Starratt (1994) noted, ideally school leaders weave these ethical paradigms together like a tapestry so that the resultant "blending . . . encourages a rich human response to the many uncertain ethical situations the school community faces every day, both in the learning tasks as well as in its attempt to govern itself" (p. 57).

Amid all of this uncertainty, one thing remains certain: digital technologies will continue to suffuse our learning, teaching, and schooling processes. Accordingly, we need to regularly identify and discuss various technology leadership scenarios so that we can try and come to agreement—at least in our local communities—about how to ethically and professionally address these incidents in ways that best serve our students and families.

Interested in further discussion on this topic? Engage with me at twitter.com/mcleod or dangerouslyirrelevant.org.

REFERENCES

American Association of School Administrators (AASA). (2018). *Statement of ethics for educational leaders*. Retrieved on December 1, 2018, from http://aasa.org/content.aspx?id=1390.

Association for Middle Level Education. (2018). *Partners*. Retrieved on December 1, 2018, from https://www.amle.org/AboutAMLE/Partners/tabid/418/undefined.

Beck, L. G. (1994). *Reclaiming educational administration as a caring profession*. New York: Teachers College Press.

Blikstein, P. (2013, June). *You cannot think about thinking without thinking about what Seymour Papert would think*. Retrieved on December 1, 2018, from https://tltl.stanford.edu/content/you-cannot-think-about-thinking-without-thinking-about-what-seymour-papert-would-think.

Colorado Department of Education. (2016). *Colorado's data privacy law*. Retrieved on December 1, 2018, from http://www.cde.state.co.us/dataprivacyandsecurity/coprivacylawtraining09282017.

Common Sense Media. (2018). *How common is cyberbullying?* Retrieved on December 1, 2018, at https://www.commonsensemedia.org/cyberbullying/how-common-is-cyberbullying.

Herold, B. (2018, July 18). *Facial recognition systems pitched as school safety solution, raising alarms*. Retrieved from Education Week on December 1, 2018, at https://www.edweek.org/ew/articles/2018/07/18/facial-recognition-systems-pitched-as-school-safety-solutions-ra.html.

International Society for Technology in Education. (2018). *ISTE standards for education leaders*. Retrieved on December 1, 2018, from https://www.iste.org/standards/for-education-leaders.

Lewis, A. (2010). *User-driven discontent* [blog comment]. Retrieved from MetaFilter on December 1, 2018, at https://www.metafilter.com/95152/Userdriven-discontent#32560467.

Malkus, N., & Cummings, A. (2018, November 27). *What we're getting wrong about credit recovery*. Retrieved from Education Week on December 1, 2018, at https://www.edweek.org/ew/articles/2018/11/27/what-were-getting-wrong-about-credit-recovery.html.

Michelson, A., Serra, R., & Weyergraf, C. (1979, Autumn). The films of Richard Serra: An interview. *October, 10*, 69–104. doi:10.2307/778630.

Molnar, A. (2005). *School commercialism: From democratic ideal to market commodity*. New York: Routledge.

Molnar, A., & Boninger, F. (2015). *Sold out: How marketing in school threatens children's well-being and undermines their education*. Lanham, MD: Rowman & Littlefield.

Mullins, L. (2018, May 21). *How schools across the country are working to detect threats made on social media*. Retrieved from National Public Radio on December 1, 2018, at https://www.npr.org/2018/05/21/613117571.

National Association of Secondary School Principals (NASSP). (2013, November). *Position statement: Ethics for school leaders*. Retrieved on December 1, 2018, from https://www.nassp.org/wordpress/wp-content/uploads/2018/07/NASSP_position-statement_Ethics.pdf.

Nicodemo, A., & Petronio, L. (2018, February 26). *Schools are safer than they were in the 90s, and school shootings are not more common than they used to be, researchers say*. Retrieved from Northeastern University on December 1, 2018, at https://news.northeastern.edu/2018/02/26/schools-are-still-one-of-the-safest-places-for-children-researcher-says.

Noddings, N. (1992). *The challenge to care in schools: An alternative approach to education*. New York: Teachers College Press.

Powell, A., Roberts, V., & Patrick, S. (2015, September). *Using online learning for credit recovery: Getting back on track for graduation*. Vienna, VA: iNACOL.

Przybylski, A. K., & Bowes, L. (2017). Cyberbullying and adolescent well-being in England: A population-based cross-sectional study. *The Lancet Child & Adolescent Health, 1*(1), 19–26. doi: 10.1016/S2352–4642(17)30011–1.

Schneier, B. (2003). *Beyond fear: Thinking sensibly about security in an uncertain world*. New York: Springer.

Schneier, B. (2018, November). *How surveillance inhibits freedom of expression*. Retrieved on December 1, 2018, from https://www.schneier.com/blog/archives/2018/11/how_surveillanc_1.html.

Schuppe, J. (2018, May). *Schools are spending billions on high-tech security. But are students any safer?* Retrieved from NBC News on December 1, 2018, at https://www.nbcnews.com/news/us-news/schools-are-spending-billions-high-tech-security-are-students-any-n875611.

Shapiro, J. P., & Stefkovich, J. A. (2016). *Ethical leadership and decision making in education: Applying theoretical perspectives to complex dilemmas* (4th ed.). New York: Routledge.

Starratt, R. J. (1994). *Building an ethical school: A practical response to the moral crisis in schools*. London: Falmer Press.

Strike, K. A. (2006). *Ethical leadership in schools: Creating community in an environment of accountability*. Thousand Oaks, CA: Corwin Press.

Watters, A. (2018, December 18). *The stories we were told about education technology (2018)*. Retrieved from Hack Education on December 20, 2018, at http://hackeducation.com/2018/12/18/top-ed-tech-trends-stories.

Wexler, N. (2018, November 29). *Why graduation rates are rising but student achievement is not*. Retrieved from Forbes on December 1, 2018, at https://.forbes.com/sites/nataliewexler/2018/11/29/why-graduation-rates-are-rising-but-student-achievement-is-not.

Glossary

1:1 initiative: A school or district computing initiative that provides a computing device for every student (i.e., 1 computer for every 1 student), either school- or district-wide or in particular grade levels, and typically allows students to take their computers home on the evenings and weekends.

Android: An operating system for mobile devices developed with leadership and support from Google (Enck, Ongtang, & McDaniel, 2009).

BYOD (Bring Your Own Device): A system where digital devices would not only be purchased by the school district, but students would also have the option to use their own smartphones and tablet computers to complete class work or access learning resources while at school (Educational Technology, 2012).

dictation software: Voice recognition software that will allow you to enter text on a computer using your voice narration and without typing (Holt, 2016).

direct instruction: A term to describe "(1) instructional approaches that are structured, sequenced, and led by teachers, and/or (2) the presentation of academic content to students by teachers, such as in a lecture or demonstration. In this type of instruction teachers are 'directing' the instructional process" (Glossary of Education Reform, n.d.).

Doceri: An interactive whiteboard app that allows the teacher to control the computer, annotate presentations, create video lessons and share in advance as a flipped classroom. "*Doceri* is known as an 'interactive whiteboard app for iPad. . . . Essentially, the *Doceri* app will allow you to view the classroom computer screen directly on your iPad. You can control the screen as if you were sitting right in front of it—advance slides, open web sites, play videos. What's more, you can use your finger (or a stylus) to draw right on your iPad screen, and everything you do is shown on the in-room projector" (University of Washington, 2017).

Dragon Dictation: A specific brand of dictation and voice recognition software (Holt, 2016).

Edmodo: A closed system so that teachers and students can communicate and share links and documents in a safe environment. This system enables teachers to share content, distribute quizzes and assignments, and manage communication with students, colleagues, and parents (Edmodo, 2012).

entrance slip: A writing assignment completed at the start of class to elicit students' thoughts about the topic, materials, or strategy before experiencing the class (University of North Carolina at Pembroke, 2017).

exit slip: A writing assignment that checks for understanding generally at the end of the instructional segment. Exit slips elicit students' thoughts about the topic, materials, or strategy after experiencing the class (University of North Carolina at Pembroke, 2017).

generative feedback: A reciprocal exchange between a giver and a receiver, where all parties are open to generating personal and systems change as a result of the feedback (Pezet, 2010).

generative responses: Students creating objects or outcomes that are the same or alike in some mathematically significant sense.

Google Classroom: A blended learning platform that "helps teachers create and organize assignments, provide feedback, and communicate with their class. Google Classroom integrates with Google Docs, Drive, and Gmail to help teachers create and collect assignments paperlessly (Google Classroom, n.d.).

Google Drive: A "beefed-up version of Google Docs" that allows users to share documents, spreadsheets, slideshows with submission ability, collaboration, and feedback. "You can store your documents, photos, music, videos, etc. all in one place. It syncs with your mobile devices and your computer, so if you make a change from one gadget, it will automatically show up if you were to access it elsewhere" (Horn, 2012).

Google Earth: A browser that accesses satellite and aerial imagery, ocean bathymetry, and other geographic data over the internet to represent the Earth as a three-dimensional globe (Pedagogy in Action, 2016).

Google for Education: "An ecology of digital tools from Google designed to host and distribute digital documents, communication, and collaboration through cloud-based technology" (TeachThought Staff, 2017).

Google Forms: An application that provides a fast way to create online surveys, with responses collected in an online spreadsheet. Survey questions can be answered from almost any web browser, including mobile smartphone and tablet browsers (Wolber, 2012).

graphic organizer: A means of communication that uses visual symbols to express knowledge, concepts, thoughts, or ideas, and the relationships between them. The main purpose of a graphic organizer is to provide a visual aid to facilitate learning and instruction. Also known as a knowledge map, concept map, story map (or storymap), cognitive organizer, advance organizer, or concept diagram (web.dote, n.d.).

guided inquiry: An approach to promoting learning through student investigation. It is designed to assist teachers in targeting higher-level thinking and science process skills for their students (Guided Inquiry Process, n.d.).

integrated technology: The integration into normal day-to-day operations of technology relevant to meeting the needs of the organization. Such integration has the potential to improve efficiency and effectiveness.

Khan Academy: A nonprofit educational organization created in 2006 to provide an accessible source of education. The organization produces short lectures in the form of YouTube videos. "Khan Academy offers practice exercises, instructional videos, and a personalized learning dashboard that empower learners to study at their own pace in and outside of the classroom." Among the subjects offered are mathematics, science, computer programming, history, art history, and economics (Khan Academy, n.d.).

key in software: A product key (also known as a software key). A specific key for a computer program that certifies that the copy of the program is original (Glossary, IT Service, n.d.).

learning goal or learning intention: A statement that describes clearly what the teacher wants the students to know, understand, and be able to do as a result of the learning and teaching activities (Assessment for Learning, n.d.).

Nearpod: A platform that engages students by sharing presentations, receiving their thinking, collecting shared information, providing instant feedback, and tracking student performance (Nearpod, n.d.).

Pinterest: A visual bookmarking tool that allows users to explore and save or "pin" creative ideas for later reference (Pinterest, 2017).

Poll Everywhere: The use of cellphones to text a response that can be displayed for formative assessment or taking attendance (Poll Everywhere, n.d.).

QR (Quick Response) codes: A two-dimensional square barcode with embedded links to information such as texts, emails, websites, phone numbers, and so on, that can be read using smartphones or other devices that are compatible with QR reading. (What is a QR code?, n.d.).

ReadWriteThink.org: A website that offers educators and students access to free high-quality resources in reading and language arts instruction. You can use this website to help students plan persuasive essays, write biographies, create timelines, and so forth (ReadWriteThink, 2017).

safe digital spaces: Online spaces that foster encouraging and constructive interactions among students when we ask students to share their ideas and take intellectual risks (Thornton, M., 2015).

scaffold (or scaffolding): A variety of instructional techniques used to move students progressively toward fuller understanding and independence in the learning process (Great Schools Partnership, n.d.).

Shadow Puppet Edu: An app that records voices and creates videos using images or resources of the user. Common Core standards and lessons are embedded in the app.

social media: "The collective of online communications channels dedicated to community-based input, interaction, content-sharing and collaboration. Websites and applications dedicated to forums, microblogging, social networking, social bookmarking, social curation, and wikis are among the different types of social media" (Rouse M., 2016a).

Socrative: A classroom tool for visualizing and measuring student understanding in real time (Socrative, n.d.).

SplashTop: An app for controlling presentations on a computer; allows for annotating, interacting, and other uses ("What is Splashtop Remote?", n.d.).

SpokenVerse: Found on YouTube. Verses that are read for understanding and enjoyment.

synchronous: From Greek syn-, meaning "with," and chronos, meaning "time," an adjective describing objects or events that are coordinated in time. In program-to-program communication, synchronous communication requires that each end of an exchange of communication respond in turn without initiating a new communication (Rouse, 2006b).

tablet: A wireless, portable personal computer with a touchscreen interface. The tablet is typically smaller than a notebook computer, but larger than a smartphone (Rouse, 2016b).

TED Talk: A nonprofit devoted to spreading ideas, usually in the form of short, powerful talks (eighteen minutes or less). TED began in 1984 as a conference where Technology, Entertainment and Design converged, and today covers almost all topics—from science to business to global issues—in more than a hundred languages (TED, n.d.).

text to speech options: Computer applications that read the text on your screen aloud.

Venn diagram: A diagram representing mathematical or logical sets pictorially as circles or closed curves within an enclosing rectangle, common elements of the sets being represented by the areas of overlap among the circles (English Oxford Living Dictionaries, n.d.).

websites: "A connected group of pages on the World Wide Web regarded as a single entity, usually maintained by one person or organization and devoted to a single topic or several closely related topics" (Dictionary.com, n.d.).

YouTube: "A free video sharing website that makes it easy to watch online videos. You can even create and upload your own videos to share with others. Originally created in 2005, YouTube is now one of the most popular sites on the Web, with visitors watching around 6 billion hours of video every month" (GCF Global, 2017).

REFERENCES FOR GLOSSARY

Assessment for Learning. (n.d.). Learning intentions. Retrieved from http://www.assessmentforlearning.edu.au/professional_learning/learning_intentions/learning_intentions_landing_page.html.

Dictionary.com. (n.d.). Websites. Retrieved October 24, 2017, from http://www.dictionary.com/browse/websites?s=t.

Edmodo. (2012). Web 2.0 tools for teachers. Retrieved from https://sites.google.com/site/kratzwilkesfinalproject/home/edmondo?tmpl=%2Fsystem%2Fapp%2Ftemplates%2Fprint%2F&showPrintDialog=1.

Education Reform. (2015).

Educational Technology. (2012). What is BYOD (Bring Your Own Device) and why should teachers care? Retrieved from http://education.cu-portland.edu/blog/tech-ed/what-is-byod-bring-your-own-device-and-why-should-teachers-care/.

Enck, W., Ongtang, M., & McDaniel, P. (2009, January/February). Understanding Android security, *IEEE Security & Privacy, 7*, pp. 50–57. doi:10.1109/MSP.2009.26.

English Oxford Living Dictionaries. (n.d.). Venn diagram. Retrieved October 24, 2017, from https://en.oxforddictionaries.com/definition/venn_diagram.

GCF Global. (2017). YouTube: What is YouTube? Retrieved from https://www.gcflearnfree.org/youtube/what-is-youtube/1/.

Glossary. "IT Service," Newcastle University. (n.d.). Retrieved from http://www.ncl.ac.uk/itservice/software/licences/glossary/.

Google Classroom. (n.d.). Retrieved from https://chrome.google.com/webstore/detail/google-classroom/mfhehppjhmmnlfbbopchdfldgimhfhfk?hl=en.

Great Schools Partnership (n.d.). *The glossary of education reform for journalists, parents, and community members*. Portland, ME. Author. Retrieved from https://www.edglossary.org/scaffolding/.

Guided Inquiry Process. (n.d.). Teaching Great Lakes science. Retrieved from http://www.miseagrant.umich.edu/lessons/teacher-tools/guided-inquiry-process/.

Holt, J. (2016, May 23). Author Joe Holt writes books using Dragon speech recognition software. Retrieved from http://whatsnext.nuance.com/office-productivity/author-writes-books-faster-with-speech-recognition-software/.

Horn, L. (2012). What is Google Drive? Gizmodo. Retrieved from http://gizmodo.com/5904653/what-is-google-drive.

Khan Academy. (n.d.). Retrieved from https://www.khanacademy.org/about.

Nearpod. (n.d.). Retrieved from https://nearpod.com/.

Pedagogy in Action. (2016). What is Google Earth? Retrieved from http://serc.carleton.edu/sp/library/google_earth/what.html.

Pezet, M. (2010). Feedback pocketbook. Laurel House, Alresford, Hants: Management Pocketbooks, Ltd., p. 19.

Pinterest. (2017). Retrieved from https://www.pinterest.com/.

Poll Everywhere. (n.d.). Retrieved from https://www.polleverywhere.com/.

ReadWriteThink. (2017). Retrieved from http://readwritethink.org/.

Rouse, M. (2006a). Asynchronous. In *SearchNetworking*. Retrieved from http://searchnetworking.techtarget.com/definition/asynchronous.

Rouse, M. (2006b). Synchronous. *TechTarget*. Retrieved from http://whatis.techtarget.com/definition/synchronous.

Rouse, M. (2016a). Social media. *TechTarget*. Retrieved from http://whatis.techtarget.com/definition/social-media.

Rouse, M. (2016b). Tablet. In *SearchMobileComputing*. Retrieved from http://searchmobilecomputing.techtarget.com/definition/tablet-PC.

Rouse, M. (2017a). Curation. *TechTarget*. Retrieved from http://whatis.techtarget.com/definition/curation.

Rouse, M. (2017b). Google Docs. Retrieved from http://whatis.techtarget.com/definition/Google-Docs.

Socrative. (n.d.). Retrieved from https://twitter.com/Socrative.

TeachThought Staff (2017). What is Google for Education? *Teach Thought*. http://www.teachthought.com/uncategorized/what-is-google-for-education/.

TED. (n.d.). About. Retrieved from https://www.ted.com/about/our-organization.

Thornton, M. (2015). *Creating space for risk*. Retrieved May 24, 2019, from https://www.edutopia.org/blog/creating-space-for-risk-michael-thornton-cheryl-harris.

University of North Carolina at Pembroke. (2017). Entrance and exit slips. Retrieved from http://www.uncp.edu/academics/opportunities-programs-resources/academic-resources/writing-across-curriculum-teaching-circle/entrance-and-exit-slips.

University of Washington. (2017). About Doceri. Retrieved from https://www.tacoma.uw.edu/teaching-learning-technology/about-doceri.

web.dote. (n.d.). Retrieved from http://web.dote.vn/kien-thuc/to-chuc-do-hoa.html.

What is a QR code? (n.d.). Retrieved from http://www.whatisaqrcode.co.uk/.

What is Splashtop Remote? (n.d.). Retrieved May 24, 2019, from https://www.shouldiremoveit.com/Splashtop-Remote-56813-program.aspx.

Wolber, A. (2012). Use Google Forms to create a survey. *TechRepublic*. Retrieved from http://www.techrepublic.com/blog/google-in-the-enterprise/use-google-forms-to-create-a-survey/.

Index

1:1 initiative, 94, 96, 111

accountability, 24, 27, 70–71, 85, 95, 107
advocacy groups, 84
American Association of School Administrators (AASA), 95, 97
Americans with Disabilities Act, 61
Andreasen, Janet B., 23–35
Android devices, 111
apps:
  for engagement in learning and thinking, 31;
  for facilitating student collaboration, 31–32
Asian American Justice Center (AAJC), 84
Asian American Legal Defense and Education Fund (AALDEF), 84
assessment:
  digitally scaffolded instruction and, 24, 26, 28, 30;
  Eduphoria *Aware*, 39–42, 45;
  equity audits, 71, 88;
  PCK and, 4, 6, 8–10, 12–14, 17–18
Association for Middle Level Education (AMLE), 97

Association for Supervision and Curriculum Development (ASCD), 34
Aware. See Eduphoria *Aware*

Badgett, Kevin, 37–47, 85
Ball, D. L., 6
Bass, H., 6
Bauer, S., 16–18
Beck, L. G., 93
Bedford School District, 94–95
Bell v. Itawamba County School Board, 57
Bethel v. Fraser, 1986, 51–52, 59, 61
Bill & Melinda Gates Foundation, 34
Blackmore, J., 70
Blikstein, P., 97
Blue Mountain v. Snyder, 59
Bolman, L., 12
Brazer, S. David, 1–19
Brooks, J. S., 71
Brown, K. M., 87
Budden, A. E., 9
Buessink v. Woodland R-IV School District, 58
bullying, 61
BYOD (Bring Your Own Device), 34, 111
Byrne-Jiménez, Mónica, ix–xi

Calvert, C., 58
capacity building, 45
Chandra, V., 18
Christman, Dana, xiii–xvi, 69–89
civil rights, 61
Cohen, E. G., 16
competencies, 5, 13, 70, 72, 75, 105
Costa, A., 88
credit recovery, 105–6
critique, 91–92, 95, 97, 101–2, 104, 106
Croft, A., 14
curriculum benchmark assessments (CBAs), 38.
    See also assessment
cyberbullying, 61, 99–100

dangerouslyirrelevant.org, 108
data-driven decision making:
    district- and campus-wide data, 39–45;
    explained, 37–38;
    grade-level and teacher-level interventions, 39;
    individual students, 42–45
data privacy, 97–98
demographics, 39–40, 43, 45, 73–74, 76
dictation software, 33, 111
differentiation of instruction, 23–24, 29, 32–33
digitally scaffolded instruction:
    assessment, 28;
    explained, 24–26;
    guided practice, 26–27;
    independent practice, 27;
    introduction to, 26;
    in practice, 28–30;
    steps, 26–28
direct instruction, 26–29, 96, 111
D.J.M. v. Hannibal, 57
Doceri, 31, 111–12
Doninger v. Niehoff, 60
Dragon Dictation, 33, 112

Edmodo, 26–27, 112
education law:
    bullying and harassment, 61;
    overview, 49–50;
    probable cause vs. reasonable suspicion, 53–54;
    student discipline, 62–63;
    student speech rights, 51–53.
    See also lawsuits; Supreme Court decisions
Eduphoria *Aware.*
    benefits, 38;
    capacity building, 45–46;
    data-driven decision making, 37–46;
    Quick Views option, 38, 40;
    screenshots, 39–45.
Enck, W., 111
entrance slip, 112
Ervin-Kassab, L., 10
Ethical Leadership and Decision Making in Education (Shapiro and Stefkovich), 92
ethics:
    of care, 93, 97, 100–101, 104–5;
    of critique, 92–93;
    of justice, 92;
    of the profession, 93–94.
Evans v. Bayer, 60
exit slip, 32, 112

Facebook, 57, 60, 99.
    See also social media
First Amendment rights, 59
Flynn, Timothy, 23–35
Forssell, Karin S., 1–19, 35
Fourth Amendment protections, 53, 62
Freeman, H., 27
Furman, G., 70–71

GAFE. *See* Google, Apps for Education
Gallimore v. Henrico, 64
generative feedback, 25, 112
generative responses, 112
Gewirtz, S., 70
Goldfarb, K. P., 70
Goldin, C., 9
Google, 26, 29, 31–32, 97–98, 112–13;

Apps for Education (GAFE), 97–98;
  Classroom, 31, 112;
  Drive, 29, 112;
  Earth, 31, 112;
  Education, 26, 112;
  Forms, 32, 113
graphic organizer, 27, 113
Green, T. L., 70–71
Grinberg, J., 70
Gronn, P., 11
Grossman, P., 6
guided inquiry, 23–24, 26, 28, 113
guided practice, 26–27, 33

Hachiya, Robert F., 49–66
Hall, H. C., 6
harassment, 50, 57, 60–62, 65–66, 100
Harris, J. B., 16
Hattie, J., 27
Hazelwood v. Kuhlmeier, 1988, 52
Herold, B., 103
Hollanders, D. A., 37
hooks, bell, 87
Huffman, J., 14
Hutton, Sondra, 106

Ianson v. Zion-Benton, 64
Individualized Education Plan / Admission, Review, Dismissal (IEP/ARD), 42–43
instructional differentiation. *See* differentiation of instruction
instructional leadership, 11–13, 18, 35, 37, 47
integrated technology, 113
International Literacy Association (ILA), 34
International Society for Technology in Education (ISTE) Standards, 95
Ivory, Gary, xiii–xvi, 69–88

J.C. v. Beverly Hills, 59
J.S. v. Bethlehem Area Sch. Dist., 57
J.S. v. Blue Mountain Sch. Dist., 57–59

key in software, 33, 113
Khan Academy, 26, 113
Klein v. Smith, 58
Klump v. Nazareth, 64
Koehler, M. J., 2, 6, 11
Kowalski v. Berkeley County Schools, 60

LaVine v. Blaine School District, 58
lawsuits:
  Bell v. Itawamba County School Board, 57;
  Bethel v. Fraser, 51–52, 59, 61;
  Blue Mountain v. Snyder, 59;
  Buessink v. Woodland R-IV School District, 58;
  D.J.M. v. Hannibal, 57;
  Doninger v. Niehoff, 60;
  Evans v. Bayer, 60;
  Gallimore v. Henrico, 64;
  Hazelwood v. Kuhlmeier, 52;
  Ianson v. Zion-Benton, 64;
  J.C. v. Beverly Hills, 59;
  J.S. v. Bethlehem Area Sch. Dist., 57;
  J.S. v. Blue Mountain Sch. Dist., 57–59;
  Klein v. Smith, 58;
  Klump v. Nazareth, 64;
  Kowalski v. Berkeley County Schools, 60;
  LaVine v. Blaine School District, 58;
  Layshock v. Hermitage Sch. Dist., 59;
  Lowery v. Euverard, 57;
  Miller v. Skumanick, 62;
  misuse of technology, 54–60;
  Morse v. Frederick, 52;
  New Jersey v. T. L. O., 53–54;
  Ponce v. Socorro, 58;
  Riley v. California, 54;
  R.S. v. Minnewaska, 64;
  Safford v. Redding, 54, 63;
  S.J.W. v. Lee's Summit R-7 Sch. Dist., 60;

Sullivan v. Houston Indep. Sch. Dist, 55;
Tinker v. Des Moines, 51–52, 55–57, 59–61;
T.V. ex rel. B.V. v. Smith-Green, 62;
Wisniewski v. Bd. of Educ., 57.
See also education law; Supreme Court decisions
Layshock v. Hermitage Sch. Dist., 59
leaders:
  BYOD and, 34;
  implementation of digital instruction, 34–35;
  resources provided by, 33–34.
League of Latin American Citizens (LULAC), 84
learning goals/intentions, xiii, 3, 71, 95
Learning Science & Literacy: Useful Background for Learning Designers, 33–34
Lewis, A., 98
Lipsky, M., xiv, 27
Lloyd, C., 11, 18
Lotan, R. A., 16
Love, N., 85
Lowery v. Euverard, 57

Madden, M., 8
Magnusson, S., 6
Malkus, N., 105
marginalization, xv, 70–71, 76, 83–84
Mayer, R. E., 25–26
McCarthy, M., 56
McCormick, Douglas, 103
McKenzie, K. B., 70–72, 75, 82, 84–86
McLeod, Scott, 91–108
Michelson, A., 98
Miles, M., 71
Miller v. Skumanick, 62
Mishra, P., 2, 6, 11
Moll, L. C., 86
Molnar, A., 98
Morse v. Frederick, 2007, 52
Mullins, L., 104

Multi-Tiered Systems of Support (MTSS) program, 94
MySpace, 58, 60

National Association for the Advancement of Colored People (NAACP), 84
National Association of Secondary School Principals (NASSP), 34
National Congress of American Indians (NCAI), 84
National Council of Teachers of English (NCTE), 34
National Council of Teachers of Mathematics (NCTM), 34
National Hispanic Education Coalition (MALDEF), 84
National Indian Education Association (NIEA), 84
National Middle School Association (NMSA), 34
National Urban League (NUL), 84
Nearpod, 26, 31, 113
Nelson, B. S., 18
New Jersey v. T. L. O., 1985, 53–54, 63–64
Nicodemo, A., 104
Noddings, N., 93

Papert, Seymour, 97
parent opt-out, 101–3
Parent Teacher Association/Organization (PTA/PTO), 84
parody threats, 56–60
Parra, J. L., xv
Pass, F., 25
Pedagogical Content Knowledge (PCK), xv, 1, 6–7, 10–13, 17
Pfeffer, J., 17
Pinterest, 32, 113
Ponce v. Socorro, 58
Powell, A., 105
Powell, Selma, 23–35
Prensky, M., 8, 35

Present Levels of Academic Achievement and Functional Performance (PLAAFPs), 43
probable cause vs. reasonable suspicion, 53–54
Przybylski, A. K., 99
Purcell, K., 8
purposeful pairs, 26–29, 113

QR (Quick Response) codes, 28–29, 114

ReadWriteThink.org 27, 114
Rehabilitation Act, 61
Rikkerink, M., xiv
Riley v. California, 54
Rittel, H. W., 6
Robinson, V., 11, 18
Rossi, P. H., 27
Rowe, K., 11, 18
Rowley, J., 5

safe digital spaces, 27, 114
Safford v. Redding, 2009, 54, 63
Scanlan, M., 70
Scheurich, 69–72, 75, 84–88
Schneier, B., 104
school safety, 103–5
Schuppe, J., 104
Scott, W. R., 17
sexting, 50, 61–63, 100–101
Shadow Puppet Edu, 33, 114
Shaked, H., xiv
Shapiro, J. P., 92–93
Shulman, L. S., 6
S.J.W. v. Lee's Summit R-7 Sch. Dist., 60
Skrla, L., 69–72, 75, 84–88
Smithson, Carol, 94–95
Snapchat, 100
Sneed, M., 61
social-emotional learning, 2
social interactions, 8
social justice, equity audits on:
analysis of data on, 76–82;
assessment, 88–89;
defined, 70;
education and, 70–71;
equity traps, 86–88;
overview, 69–72;
percentages and, 72–75, 83;
in practice, 70–71;
small populations, 83–84;
steps toward equity, 84–86;
using Excel pivot tables to evaluate, 72–76.
See also ethics
social media, 50, 52, 54–57, 60–66, 99, 103–4, 114.
See also Facebook
social science, 2, 9, 28, 31
Socrative, 26, 114
SplashTop, 31, 114
SpokenVerse 33, 114
Starratt, R. J., 107
State of Texas Assessments of Academic Readiness (STAAR), 39
Stefkovich, J. A., 92–93
Stein, M. K., 18
Strike, K. A., 92
Student Data Transparency and Security Act (Colorado), 98
students:
bullying, harassment, and threats, 61;
data privacy and commercialism, 97–99;
discipline, 62–63;
learning and credit recovery, 105–6;
on-campus and off-campus behaviors, 55–56;
social media and parody threats, 56–60;
speech rights, 52–53, 56–60;
student searches, 53–54, 63–64;
technology access, 94–95;
technology use, 96–97
Sullivan v. Houston Indep. Sch. Dist., 55
Supreme Court decisions:
related to student searches, 53–54;
related to student speech, 51–53.

See also education law; legal issues
synchronous communication, 114

tablets, 31, 33, 114.
    See also BYOD
Taggart, Horace, 100–101
Taylor, Rosemarye T., 23–35
Technological Content Knowledge, 9–10
Technological Pedagogical Content Knowledge (TPACK), xv, 1;
    explained, 2;
    knowledge development and, 10;
    PCK and, 6–7;
    professional development and, 12–14;
    supporting understanding, 16–18;
    teacher expertise and, 10–11
technology access, 94–95
Technology Knowledge (TK), 7–8
technology security, 101–3
technology use, 96–97
TED Talks, 26, 114
test scores, 94–97
text to speech, 33, 115.
    See also Dragon Dictation

Theoharis, G., 70
Timberland School District, 101–2
Tinker v. Des Moines, 1969, 51–52, 55–57, 59–61
T.V. ex rel. B.V. v. Smith-Green, 62

U.S. Department of Education Office of Civil Rights (OCR), 61

Valencia, R. R., 86
Vallejo, Amanda, 97–98
Van Lare, M., 16
Venn diagrams, 7, 26–29, 115

Watters, A., 103
Weatherly, R., xiv
Weatherspoon, George, 99
websites, defined, 115
Wexler, N., 105
What I Need (WIN) class, 96
Whole Child Initiative, 97
Williams, Daryl, 97–98
Wisniewski v. Bd. of Educ., 57

Yeager, D. S., 10
YouTube, 26, 33, 57, 59, 114, 115

About the Contributors

Janet B. Andreasen, PhD, is an associate lecturer of mathematics education at the University of Central Florida (UCF). She is the coordinator of secondary education and works with prospective and practicing mathematics teachers at the elementary, middle, and high school levels.

Dr. Kevin Badgett is an associate professor and coordinator for the Educational Leadership Program at the University of Texas Permian Basin.

S. David Brazer (PhD, Stanford University) is the director of Leadership Degree Programs at Stanford University's Graduate School of Education.

Mónica Byrne-Jiménez is associate professor in the Department of Education Leadership & Policy Studies at Indiana University. She is AERA Division A vice president and UCEA past-president.

Dr. Dana Christman is an associate professor in the Department of Educational Specialties at Austin Peay State University.

Timothy Flynn received his doctor of education degree from the University of Central Florida. He currently serves as an assistant principal at Westridge Middle School in Orlando, Florida.

Karin S. Forssell directs the Learning, Design & Technology Program at Stanford University's Graduate School of Education.

Robert F. Hachiya is an associate professor in the Educational Leadership-Department of the College of Education at Kansas State University.

Gary Ivory is retired from New Mexico State University.

Scott McLeod, JD, PhD, is an associate professor of educational leadership at the University of Colorado Denver and the founding director of the University Council for Educational Administration (UCEA) Center for the Advanced Study of Technology Leadership in Education (CASTLE).

Selma Powell is director of the Special Education Teacher Education Program at the University of Washington.

Rosemarye T. Taylor is a member of the educational leadership faculty at the University of Central Florida.

About the Editors

Gary Ivory is retired from New Mexico State University. He has held a variety of leadership roles in PK–12 and postsecondary education.

Dr. Dana Christman is an associate professor in the Department of Educational Specialties at Austin Peay State University. She has held a variety of leadership roles in postsecondary education.

About the Reviewers

Roseanne Bensley has over thirty-five years' experience in student affairs and career services and in May 2018 completed her PhD in educational leadership and administration from New Mexico State University.

Krista Garcia has been a teacher, academic dean, assistant principal, and principal and is currently the director of special education in Northside Independent School District in San Antonio, Texas.

Gina Hochhalter is an instructor of English at Clovis Community College, New Mexico. She holds an EdD in educational leadership and administration from New Mexico State University.

Dr. Glenn Malone provides oversight of assessment, accountability, special education, Title I, LAP, and health services in the Puyallup School District. He has also been an adjunct professor.

Professor A. William Place is the Department Chair of Educational Leadership and Counselor Education at Eastern Kentucky University.

Dr. Roland Rios is director of technology for the Ft. Sam Houston Independent School District in San Antonio, Texas. He has been a math teacher, secondary principal, and assistant principal.

Dr. Arsenio Romero is superintendent of Deming Public Schools and has been an assistant superintendent in curriculum. He holds a doctorate in educational leadership and administration from New Mexico State University.

Dr. Steven Sánchez is currently a multiage middle-grades teacher for the Los Lunas Family School. He has been an interim superintendent, deputy superintendent, and a program director for the National Science Foundation.

Abigail Tarango is director of Special Projects & Strategic Initiatives for the Ysleta Independent School District in El Paso, Texas. She is a doctoral candidate at New Mexico State University.

www.ingramcontent.com/pod-product-compliance
Lightning Source LLC
Chambersburg PA
CBHW051814230426
43672CB00012B/2726